A NEW LOOK IN PREACHING

A New Look in Preaching

BY

JAMES A. PIKE

BISHOP OF CALIFORNIA

The George Craig Stewart
Memorial Lectures
at Seabury-Western Theological
Seminary

NEW YORK

CHARLES SCRIBNER'S SONS

*To two early mentors in content
and the communication thereof*

CHARLES W. F. SMITH

and

HOWARD A. JOHNSON

*Priests and Doctors
of the Holy Catholic Church*

TABLE OF CONTENTS

PREFACE

These lectures were given at an Episcopal seminary by an Episcopal priest talking about preaching in his own Church. In the writing I gave serious thought to broadening the scope to eliminate any special "denominational flavor." I I have resisted the temptation, because the whole approach is toward the *specific*. To put everything in generalizations might seem to give the work a broader application on problems of preaching throughout the Christian Church, but actually to focus upon the problem in terms of a particular Church may throw more light on the problem in other Churches (and I presume that this problem does exist in other Churches) than a generic approach.

I do really hope that some non-Episcopal readers will stick with the book and in the process do an additional job of "translation" (its main theme): how do these concerns apply in terms of my task, my people, with a different liturgy, with a different degree of preparation re the Bible, etc. In short, what can I learn from the malaise—and the opportunity—of the Episcopal Church in regard to this central matter of communication of the Gospel?

Such readers outside of my own Church as are willing to go through this exercise are cordially invited—indeed beseeched—to write me their reactions, particularly as to the applicability of some of these things to their own Communions. Many of us have said much about the value of sharing our "best" in the coming Great Church (to use Canon Wedel's fine phrase); but actually our hearts may be found closer together as we share our problems —even our weaknesses. In any case, I want to say with all honesty that in my speaking of terms of our own Communion, I have not meant to exclude the non-Anglican reader.

The opportunity to express my ideas on this important subject was provided to me by the invitation of the Rev. Canon Alden D. Kelly, then President and Dean of Seabury-Western Theological Seminary. His initial courtesy, expressed in his invitation to me to undertake the task, was fulfilled by his successor, the Very Rev. Charles U. Harris —who, with his wife, provided both encouragement and hospitality in the doing thereof.

Sometimes style takes second place to passion. This is true in the case of this book. There is something here to be said. How it is said is another question. The substance of these pages represents the result of my thinking and practice over a good many years. Concerning the form, I want to say that the professional may find what is written here to be in quite simple, direct language, but the fact that a "fresh" (in both the dictionary and the slang sense of the word) approach still permeates these pages, may not be entirely a drawback. Freshness is part of my thesis as to how we should preach these days. The style (more informal than any I have allowed to go into printed pages before) is a sample of what I recommend for preaching—each man taking the hint in his own way. Actually, in preaching and lecturing I use even plainer speech than this; in fact in odd moments of time, I have tried to "dress up" this piece of writing because of my admiration for the high standards of the Seminary which sponsored the lectures and the publisher who is putting them between hard covers.

Since, after seeing the manuscript, the Seminary was still willing to sponsor it and the publisher was still willing to publish it, I can now be bold enough to say that I have two prejudices (or are they?): (1) many things said in seminaries for the training of preachers mislead them into too elegant a mode of discourse; and (2) many things published for professionals similarly mislead them. Actually, I am grateful for the respect for fine language on the part both of seminary professors and of religious editors; but I am still worried about the people on whom elegant language is pressed. I know that many of you are too; hence I have made bold to put this out under my name.

If those to whom you are ministering are able to receive a more classical form of discourse than this represents, either stop reading the book or "upgrade" this material to their level. If, on the other hand, the only problem is that you are used to a more elegant level of discourse than this represents, and than your people are used to, then it might be just as well that you read it right through. I can talk and write differently, as some of you know; but here it happens that I am not so doing. The author would simply take his justification from I Corinthians 12, were it not for the fact that St. Paul left out one important thing. In that passage he did not make mention of the diversity in the same person, given different purposes at different times.

JAMES A. PIKE

The Cathedral Close
San Francisco
Whitsuntide, 1961

A NEW LOOK IN PREACHING

THE CONCERN OF THIS BOOK

OF COURSE I am most honored to be in the goodly succession of those who have occupied this lectureship and especially to be associated with the name of the great Bishop Stewart, whom I have long admired and who really was a *preacher*. Your good Faculty and previous Dean obviously apparently did not inspect a transcript of my seminary study; otherwise I never should have been invited: I managed to secure a Bachelor of Divinity degree without ever having taken a course in homiletics or preaching. But I have had to do some of it in recent years and hence make bold to speak quite informally to you as to some of my concerns about preaching: mostly to raise problems, rather than to announce answers.

Since I am talking about preaching in an age of transition, it would be well to start with some discussion of what has been happening to the hearers. Then I will move to *what* we are trying to communicate and *how* we might well communicate it in the light of the transition in the hearers. Third, I will turn to the preacher himself and his preparation for his task. Then, last, I will address myself to the context of the preaching, i.e., the relationship of preaching to the Liturgy.

In modern merchandising terms, we might call the first task a "market survey." The second we might call an analysis of the "product" and its "packaging." In the third and fourth sections we turn to "the salesman" and "the store."

The Church should be more and more concerned with assessment of those to whom it is doing its talking. That should have much to do with how we say it. None of this affects the product: any relativism or pragmatism you note in the first chapter should not disturb you too much; I am not going to be relativistic about what we are seeking to market. But I will be relativistic and pragmatic as to *how* to market it.

Once on Trinity Sunday I heard a brilliant sermon by a young curate. He began, "I wish to explain to you this afternoon the doctrine of the most blessed and glorious Trinity." He began with the relationship of the Three Persons before the beginning of time. He developed this most carefully and in the most orthodox manner. But I'm sure nothing at all got through to the bulk of his hearers. There is nothing more irrelevant than answers to questions people haven't asked: I doubt if there was a person in that congregation who was the least anxious about what had been the relationship of the members of the Holy Trinity before Creation.

Now it very well may be that what various theologians have worked out on this subject would have a bearing on things about which people are concerned, but no such connection was made.

At the other extreme, several years ago a distinguished urban rector who believed in "relevant preaching" preached on the subject of the Holy Trinity too, and he quickly came down to the existential level. Right at the time Britain, United States, Russia and China had combined against the German-Japan axis he said, in effect, "Now, this is the feast of the blessed Trinity. This is a very difficult concept. I think we will understand it better if we analyze what has happened in the world in the fact of this Nazi terrorism. Now, this is very much like the theological problem. There is Great Britain, the old, the venerable, the ancient, just like God the Father; there is the United States, active, articulate, expressive, like God the Son; there is Russia, imaginative, looking into the future —God the Holy Ghost. And there's China—but I'll advert to it next Sunday."

The difficulty with that form of "relevance" (and he never got back to the theology at all) is illustrated by the fact that after our falling out with Russia he felt compelled to take as his text on Good Friday "Christ or Barabbas?", identifying the

United States with Christ and Russia with Barabbas. (This is quite a come-down after he'd been the Holy Ghost.)

Herein lies our problem. Much preaching errs either in presenting the real thing, the true faith, in a way that nobody cares about it, or in levelling off everything so that the answers are in no higher terms than the questions. Our problem is how to communicate the Faith in terms of the questions people care about, providing answers rephrased and rethought—not changed, but repackaged. This is the concern of this book.

CHAPTER I

MARKET SURVEY

No INTELLIGENT producer these days will put a product on the market without a market survey. Professionals who conduct these surveys study cross-sections of the public and seek to discern what approaches in advertising and packaging will make the product most saleable. As our Lord pointed out: "The children of this world are in their generation wiser than the children of light": if it is important to consider the "market" in the case of the contemplated promotion of a new detergent, it is certainly important as we plan the propagation of the Gospel. What follows is not a complete "market survey"; it is simply a sketchy illustration of the types of considerations we should bear in mind as a foundation for planning the presentation of our message. In short, it is a brief analysis of the people to whom we are talking, intended to yield some clues as to how we ought to talk.

The factors which bear on the life of the hearers in our time can be summarized under four headings:

1. Remnants of old factors;

2. Trends which are unfavorable—which create difficulty for our task;

3. Trends which are neutral—which are neither good nor bad in themselves, but are just there to cope with; and

4. Trends which are favorable—which ease fulfillment of our task.

1. *Remnants of old factors*

First, there is still a remnant of the fact that we were a frontier country: a protest against the formal. Many of those whom we would reach outside the Church, many who have lapsed from other groups of Christians, and even many who are within the Church, are still anti-formal, in varying degrees. At first they don't take too well to a liturgical church and are put off by "form" and ceremonial. (By the way, many of such don't know anything about high or low church; low church looks high to them—"fancy—and things going on.")

This problem is diminishing and we are making progress, in some circles. Many of the *nouveau riche* (and this covers half the population these days) as a result of more extensive education and "advantages" are becoming more sensitive than their parents were to esthetic things—to beauty of language, to form. But there is still a strong remnant of this resistance.

In the fourth chapter, I will talk about the positive value of the liturgy in communication. But as for reaching the people by preaching, the service is sort of a roadblock to people who view it, in relation to the sermon, as very similar to the reading of the minutes of the last meeting. And that is precisely what many feel the service is; they figure we must go through this form before we can have the real thing. (It is no accident that in churches where the preaching is more obviously the main thing the place where the people sit is called the "auditorium"—a place in which to *hear* something.)

This means that our preaching in the Episcopal Church has to be *better* to counteract resistance to what else goes on in the service—until the newcomers come to understand and love the liturgy. We've got to preach so well that they will *even* come to the service because they want to hear the sermon, until they come to realize, from our preaching and otherwise, that they want to come to the service, even if the sermon is a poor one.

A second remnant of the old factors in American life is anti-intellectualism. There has been some diminution of this spirit since Sputnik was launched and we have pondered seriously the

educational system of the Russians as compared
with ours. As someone said, "What we need in
this country is more eggheads and fewer fatheads."
And yet, in spite of continuing evidence of Soviet
educational superiority in some realms, there is
still in many quarters a resistance to looking too
bright. It happens in colleges as well as in high
schools. The boy who knows the answer and puts
up his hand is apt to be looked down upon by his
fellows. In some quarters you've got to look dumb
in order to be popular. This reaction-pattern is a
roadblock to us. We have been among those
Churches who take most seriously the intellectual
tradition in Christendom. And we have been
somewhat at a disadvantage because of it.

Speaking of education, a third factor—one that
has been operative for a long time—is the secularism of education. The world-view communicated
can perhaps best be called *secularism by default*.
The number of teachers in our colleges and schools
who have deliberately set out to make atheists of
our children are very few indeed. The real danger
is an unconscious influence operating during the
working hours of the pupil: the impression that
you can sufficiently explain life by talking about
man and things without God, flesh without spirit,
time and history without eternity. And the teachers don't ignore the eternal dimension of reality

because they're against it. This teacher may be a psalm-singing Christian, a Sunday School teacher or even a tither. It's just that the rules of the game say that we mustn't talk about it—it's "divisive." And hence, there's not been a neutral result; there's been a sectarian result. By default there has been communicated the impression which is precisely that desired by the consciously convinced secularist; and secularism is, of course, in itself a religion, i.e., a world-view taken by faith.

As a result partly of the educational process, partly of the general neglect of the family life in its old-fashioned corporate sense and partly of the real decrease of the place of the Church in people's lives—there is a fourth factor. The fact is that most of our people know nothing whatsoever about the Bible (or, for that matter, about the history of the Christian Church). This, too, is a road-block to our preaching. The passing allusions made in many of our sermons to Biblical history, parables, or the lives of the Saints are often a waste of time. The hearers never heard of them, they know nothing about them. This means that we must either omit such references or take the time to tell the people the whole thing from the beginning, including its real meaning in terms of its context—from what we know from biblical criticism, and not in some unconsciously funda-

mentalistic way because we want to say it quickly.
It takes longer to be a non-fundamentalist about
some of these passages in the Bible, let alone the
meaning of incidents in Church history. It is
quicker to say: "St. John said . . ." than to say "The
unknown author of the fourth Gospel said . . ."
It is easier to say "Adam and Eve in the Garden
. . ." rather than to explain the mythological—and
true—meaning of the Edenic narrative.

Some years ago I was quite thrilled to be up on
Mt. Carmel, overlooking the port of Haifa, where
Elijah had it out with the priests of Baal. With
enthusiasm I mentioned this experience to a
group at a party in New York soon after my return.
Their response to my biblical reference was, in
effect, "Who did what to whom?" They hadn't the
remotest idea about any of it.

I appreciate this point more than most Episcopal
clergy because of a lack in my own background. I
was raised a Roman Catholic. Bible reading was
rarely a part of the Roman Catholic personal or
family life. I went to seminary after I was or-
dained. When I was in the Navy I was studying
privately for Holy Orders while serving on the
secret desk in Naval Intelligence. In between the
arrival of dispatches, especially on the night shift,
much of the time I was reading away, as was my
secretary, a yeoman who was studying for the

ministry of a fundamentalist Baptist group. We weren't aware of our mutual plans the first few weeks, but finally we found out about each other's hopes. I noticed that he had only one book and I had many. He remarked, "Lt. Pike, I think you will find that the Bible will throw a lot of light on those commentaries."

This self-confession is meant to underline the fact that when we, as professionals, *assume* biblical knowledge on the part of laity, we are quite wrong. And the same is true—even more so—of the history of the Church.

One final factor is the widespread dissociation of religion from important areas of life in the view of many laymen. For all too many, religion is not supposed to have anything to do with what really matters. Having occasionally made statements on public issues, I have learned from my "negative fan-mail" over the years that the articulated objection of the layman is not so much that he disagrees with you on what you said (though he wouldn't have written if he didn't disagree), but that you said anything.

I am not going to talk about the social gospel as such; my interest here is that it does represent an important avenue of communication. We can often communicate vitally by addressing ourselves to a public question, not only because we should be talking about that question from the point of view of ethics, but also because it is a way of getting to the theology with a relevant starting point —quite apart from our responsibility to exercise our prophetic ministry, the obligation we have to face plainly a given issue.

So much for remnants of old factors. Now we turn to more recently emerging factors.

2. *Trends which are unfavorable*

Here I will first "file by title," as we lawyers say. There are two important books to read. If you have not read them, they are at this point, in terms of immediate relevance, almost as important as reading the Bible. They will help us in understanding those to whom we are seeking to bring the biblical message.

One is *The Organization Man*[1] and the other is *The Hidden Persuaders.*[2] The first book tells you about the way life has become *organized* around unconsciously held secularist ideas, the way conformity has replaced that independence and freedom of spirit which has been our very meat, the way that life has become so blueprinted that there isn't much room for the highest levels of

[1] By William H. Whyte, Jr. (Simon & Schuster).
[2] By Vance O. Packard (McKay). See also his more recent *The Status Seekers* (McKay) and *The Waste Makers* (McKay).

individuality, and the way the blueprint includes a churchly pious aspect (as long as it's in its place).

The second book covers the *methodology* of creating conformists and molded people.

These books describe processes which are in fact at work; and since our message depends essentially upon human freedom (we can't talk about sin or grace, except in terms of freedom), that which constricts and binds man and reduces the area of his freedom, is a threat to the capacity of men to receive the message and hence increases the problem of communicating it relevantly.

Second, certain trends in education are a threat to us. Less and less has there been any education in the realm of ideas and concepts. "How-to-do-it" has occupied more and more of the task. Abstract thought is pretty much gone.

The odd thing is that in past periods of American culture when the number of people college-educated or high-school-educated was fewer, still there was sufficient interest in the material of theology, there was sufficient leisure free from the distractions of television and the automobile, sufficient reading of the Bible, sufficient gathering of the family around to talk about serious things, that a kind of culture was kept up. Men talked seriously over the cracker barrel even about sub-lapsarian versus supra-lapsarian predestination.

We can laugh at that and say the issue was silly, but at least they were talking about *God*, and they were talking about intellectual concepts in logical order. Yet many of these people may not have gone beyond grade school, if that much.

Years ago I participated in a seminar on the writings of certain American preachers and theologians and spent a good deal of time on the sermons of Jonathan Edwards. I found that they required very close attention: I had to read the long sentences over and over again to get the meaning of the structure of thought. Often I had to go back and retrace the argument. Yet these highly conceptual sermons, which are today difficult for a seminarian or minister to grasp without hard work, were preached to ordinary laypeople with telling evangelistic effect. No one of us could talk anything like that: our people just won't get it —due to the fact that we have slipped so badly in our capacity for logical thought and the reception of ideas and concepts.

The last point I will mention as an unfavorable trend, is the conscious growth of a self-serving approach to religion. Of course, all through Judaeo-Christian history there have been some people seeking to "use" God. From the writings of the Old Testament on we see the condemnation of the attempt to manipulate God; so obviously there must have been attempts to do it. But now we have an "out in the open" pragmatism about religion. Among the resources which make a good life, among the things you can count on, is also God. He is offered in well-selling religious books, over the radio and television, and in some pulpits, as a resource among resources; a sleeping pill, a shot in the arm, or tranquilizer—depending upon the particular need (real or supposed) of the individual. I am surprised that we have not yet had a book entitled *How to Be Like Yourself—and Like Yourself*. The implication of all this is "You are the Center; God is on the periphery, to be turned to from time to time and utilized." Obviously the heart of our message is that God is not to be used, but to be adored and served. But according to the apostles of this trend, you are to be the center of worship and He the acolyte.

All this expresses itself on the national level too. A prominent national group of patriots says, "Let's get back to God." (This "get back to" is ambiguous, because in the "good old days," 15% of the Americans were connected with Churches, and today 63.4% are; on the other hand, more families were reading the Bible and those who were church-affiliated were generally more serious about it all.) And so often we hear that religion is a great bulwark against Communism. It is; but such statements generally overlook the fact that God is more important than either the United

States or Russia and will still be around when there is neither.

Here we must be very careful in our preaching: we can't flatly negate this sort of thing, without recognizing the obvious point that there is a cause and effect relationship here between our being rooted in the Ultimate Ground of Being and personal integration (and, for that matter, keeping the nation safe). If my life has been reoriented around God, my anxieties will probably be less intense, I probably *will* sleep better, my personality might become more attractive, I will probably be more successful. And certainly a nation that trusts in God and orients its purposes around His purposes will doubtless be stronger and safer as against the Communists. And it is true that God desires our health and well-being—private and corporate. There is a thin line between blasphemy, where God is being "used," and a thankful recognition of the fruits of devotion to God. Jesus said, "Seek ye the Kingdom of God and His righteousness and all these other things will be added to you"; but we have to watch out that we don't say "seek ye the Kingdom of God *in order* that these things will be added to you."

3. *Trends which are neutral*

There are a number of factors which are a challenge to us but which are not necessarily bad in themselves. First, there has been a marked change in the lingo which people use and hence in the currency in which the Gospel must be passed on. This has already been suggested in connection with the mention of the decrease in conceptual thinking.

There are basically only two ways of thinking: the Hebrew way and the Greek way. The Greek way is in terms of nouns—abstract concepts, "universals." The Hebrew way is in terms of verbs—specific action. You find little discussion in the Bible about the omnipresence, omniscience, etc., of God. Instead there is the personal testimony that "should ten thousand fall beside me," He'll be there. He's been where I've needed Him. The Bible affirms the mighty acts of God—verbs. But the Fathers who formulated the Creeds and most other theologians have thought in terms of nouns. This is why we sometimes end up with such abstract phrases in the Creeds as "of one substance with the Father." If one must ask the question, "Is Jesus Christ ὁμοούσιος or is he ὁμοιούσιος," ὁμοούσιος is the answer—of one substance, not just of like substance. But who would think of asking such a question today? I've never had a layman come up and ask it. Why? Because we have passed that particular period of thinking, and we're back again in verb-thinking; most of our people are verb-thinkers. A thing is what it does; *not*, a thing will do what it is. That is the difference. Take our vernacular. I think occasionally we can use slang in our sermons; but whether or not we want to use it, depending on our degree of dignity, at least we ought to study it. Think of the characteristic phrases people use: "What gives?" "What goes on here?" *not* "what is the essence of this?" "What is the nature of that?"

In modern thinking, we don't know what a "substance" is—neither in physics nor in spiritual things. We *do* know what the early Fathers were trying to say, and, in the light of the way the question was put, they were right. But on the same subject we should be saying to our people something like this: When you are dealing with Jesus, you're dealing with God. When you are in the hands of Jesus, you're in the hands of God. What you see in Jesus, you can trust is in God. What you hear from Jesus, you're hearing from God. Now, if we worded the Creed like that, it would lengthen the service even more; and, further, a thousand years from now, that language probably would be just as out of date. So I'm not suggesting this as a revision; anyway, we can't get a quorum any more.

To what degree we must be permanently loyal to phrases and concepts of a different era, I will discuss in the next chapter. But I am suggesting that now people talk and think less and less in a way that leaves intelligible such phrases as "of one substance with the Father." If I were asked whether I believe that phrase in the Creed, the answer would be "yes and no." I believe most firmly in the realities which the Church was asserting in these phrases; but as to the phrases, they are part of the passing era in which they were devised. God did not dictate the phrases; they are the fruit of man's concepts—and concepts now dated.

Now what is involved is not just change of words; it isn't a question of translating word for word some of the ancient formulae (or, for that matter, the Elizabethan phrases in the Prayer Book) into more modern forms. In many cases that might be useful; but it wouldn't get at the basic problem. Our people have a whole different conceptual arrangement of things—different set of pigeon holes, arranged differently. This is true even in the problem of translation from one modern language to another. You can't translate things word for word. And when fifteen centuries have passed we have to face the fact of an almost complete change in conceptual structure, not just a problem of archaism of words. This change isn't bad in itself. But it is a challenge to us in the way we talk to people. It means we have to translate not only words but concepts.

For example: Lay people who have never taken

a course in depth psychology understand nevertheless through paperback editions—and ordinary
social conversation—the lingo of depth psychology
better than they do that of traditional theology.
Here we can take a leaf from St. Thomas Aquinas.
He was impressed by the fact that many of the
thinking people of his day were talking like Aris-
totelians. Through the Crusades, the West re-
vived its touch with the writings of Aristotle,
which the Moslems had preserved, and Aristotle
had become quite the rage in the universities—
something like existentialism today. So, he bap-
tized Aristotle—the "going" philosophy—and used
it as his means of analysis and communication—and almost got declared a heretic for his
pains.

When a few years ago in the encyclical *Humani
generis* the Pope permanently froze St. Thomas
Aquinas' system and said, in effect, you must
think about theology the way he thought in the
thirteenth century, I am sure that in Heaven
there was no one more surprised than St. Thomas.
The encyclical was directly at odds with what his
whole spirit and method had been. It was: let's
speak to our age and through its lingo. And in the
Thomistic spirit, we should be talking to our
people in, for example, the terms of the categories
of depth psychology, not because we think those

categories infallible, but because through them we can better get through to people; then we can move from that to the old labels, after they once understand the content.

Second, there has been a great change in the center of interest (which the emphasis on psychological categories reflects). People are much more interested in *persons*, and less interested in ideas. Especially the centering of concern around the problem of anxiety means a difficult job of translation for us.

Third, there is an enormous mobility of population, which means that in our teaching program, in our sermon series, in our arrangements for getting to people, we have to take account of the fact that our contact is often of limited duration. In some settings we must present the whole package at once; for we have no assurance of repetition of attendance. I was particularly placed in this regard: we gave up the idea of series (except for the six weeks of University summer sessions) in a place like the New York Cathedral where there was an 85% turnover every Sunday.* There's just no use in saying "next Sunday I'll wind this up." They won't be there.

But even in regular parishes you cannot assume

* This is almost equally true of Grace Cathedral, San Francisco, where my seat now is.

that people have heard all the fundamentals. Even in what would seem today to be a fairly stable locality, you almost have to go over the same ground every year. This is quite different from the old days when people and the parson were there fifty years and the latter was expected to produce something utterly original every Sunday. Now, he can be relieved a little of that burden. He does better to keep re-plowing the field.

4. *Trends which are favorable*

First, the actual growth of the Church. One can evaluate the so-called "religious revival" in many ways. I think we can't be too sanguine about it. I think that from the statistics we should not assume that the Kingdom is just around the corner; nor can we regard the statistics as assurance that all these new people are converted Christians. On the other hand, I am not among the total debunkers of this rapid growth,[1] because this much is true: more people than ever before are now within *hearing* distance; more people are around, and who knows: more may be saved, and maybe through us. So the challenge to the preacher— and his opportunity—is all the greater than twenty

[1] Since the lectures were delivered, it would appear that the rate of growth has somewhat tapered off. *Cf.* my article, "Christianity in Retreat" in *Look*, Dec. 20, 1960.

or thirty years ago; then there weren't so many
to hear.

More than this, apart from those who are
coming, among many of those who are not coming there is a new openness. More people are
talking about ultimate problems, and sometimes in
specifically religious terms.

Particularly is this true on the campus. A somewhat wooden-minded layman on the council of a
diocese, during the discussion of the Church's
college chaplaincy program, raised the question:
"Well, is this program worth it? Just how many
conversions have there been? Precisely how many
have been brought to confirmation?" Whatever the
answer, the question wasn't the basic one. The
important thing is that there is a new temper on
the campus due to the work of the Church and
other influences; there is a great deal more openness, there are many "fellow-travellers" in Christianity. And right now, they are more valuable to
our cause than the sort of stick-in-the-mud person
who has always been what he was raised, but who
couldn't care less about ultimate questions. People
are inquiring, thinking, and looking—"fringers," if
you wish. And this is a great chance for us if we can
speak to them in a way which does not offend their
usually high degree of intellectual honesty and
at the same time attract them with a certain sweet

reasonableness (to use Bishop Stephen Bayne's phrase) which will inspire faith.

There is even beyond this open group, those who are "fellow-travellers," many now who will read books about these questions because religion has now really become an intellectual fad. At the same time—and part of the reason for this—there is the cynicism about boot-strap-lifting salvation. The old self-confident, "onward and upward" spirit ("EXCELSIOR" on every Senior Class pin) is pretty much out. Among all but the materialistically complacent and the indifferent, what we have is either *faith* or *despair*. The in-between has not settled itself. Our greatest rival, as a positive faith in the past—humanistic optimism—is now well-nigh dead.

And one final point. Favorable to our preaching are the recent events. It has suddenly dawned upon our people that we are really threatened with systemization. That to face the Soviet threat, with the obvious progress the Russians have made and their obvious efficiency, some kind of marching in ranks in our economic system, in our recruiting for industry and in our educational system, may be called for. This has caused many to worry about the degree to which we will have personal freedom.

Several years ago, it was naively said—by great

people too—that we needn't worry about Russian science, because advanced science cannot exist under an authoritarian system. But, as St. Thomas Aquinas said quite wisely, you cannot deny possibility in the face of actuality. Now the question is changed. As Reinhold Niebuhr put it, on a telecast, the question now appears to be, can you have advanced scientific development *without* authoritarianism?

The answers for human freedom in the face of the threat of the domination of *things* are still in the same old place, but we've got to bring them out, and the fact that they are relevant again so poignantly and sharply is an advantage.

I would like to out-Bultmann Bultmann, for a moment. As you know, Dr. Rudolf Bultmann has pointed out, and quite rightly, that many things in the New Testament presuppose a world-view that is not our world view—and one that wasn't true. For example, take the passage in Ephesians where St. Paul worries about astrology. He thought in common with sophisticated and unsophisticated Gentiles of his day that there were things floating up there that determined our destiny—particularly the κοσμοκράτορες—the malignant, evil "world rulers." And, believing this, the Apostle tries to point out the problem is bigger than just a matter of human negotiation: "We

wrestle not just against flesh and blood"; we
wrestle with these great sub-human things which
threaten to run us: sub-human, but "principalities
and powers."

Bultmann points out this wasn't so: those things
weren't up there. That's right, they weren't. St.
Paul was wrong. But his illusion has suddenly become very relevant. But, now, through the use of
our human freedom, we've *put* them there. And
those things up there are not simply things we've
got; they're things which *have got us*. Their presence moves into every area of life; so we've got
to do this and got to do that. And if we're going
to catch up and pass up, there's a lot we've got
to do together. And all this threatens our freedom.

You can only get a lot of people moving in the
same direction at the same time through either of
two methods—the only two the world has ever
known. One is, you're whipped together from the
outside; the other is, you're drawn together from
the inside. Today we've got to see the problem of
freedom, within the threat of domination, in those
big terms. Not just a summit conference, individual people talking and deciding—flesh and
blood; there is something else—less than human
(but which we—as human beings—have made)
in the picture.

What then is the clue? What is the way of

discipline and sacrifice which can enable a man to remain free? We know, for St. Paul gives it in the Epistles. And here the passage in the Epistle is in its description true for the first time; and the author's answers are true answers. My point here is, this new consciousness of the new threat to freedom is a good thing for our preaching: our answers are entirely relevant to that threat. This, as we will see in the fuller development of this sermon idea later, really means that we are "doing business at the same old stand."

CHAPTER II

THE PRODUCT
AND ITS PACKAGING

W_{HEN} I was a boy I had a particular
fondness for "Log Cabin Syrup." I was attracted
first by the facsimile cabin which formed its container; but I came to love the syrup as well. For
years I hadn't seen any syrup of that particular
brand until a few weeks ago when I saw on the
table at home a container of quite undistinguished
shape but with the same brand name on the label.
I tried it and found that the same familiar flavor
was there—though, for reasons best known to the
processor, a much simplified container had been
adopted.

In connection with material things we can quite
readily make the distinction between a product
and its packaging. It is somewhat more difficult
in the case of spiritual things. As touching the
Gospel, what is permanent and unchanging and
what is transient and subject to alteration or even
compromise? Sometimes those who talk about
loyalty to "the Faith" really mean loyalty to a particular form of human words or symbols which

One who involves Himself in the course of history and in our personal lives. To those who do not already grasp this, Christ is preached in vain. Or to put it in another way, the Messiah will not be accepted unless He is expected. The main problem is not convincing people that Jesus is the Messiah, but helping them see the relevance of the fact. There is no use talking redemption to a man who doesn't know he needs redeeming, or, for that matter, to one who has no sense of having anything to do about himself.

One reason for the rapid success of the Apostles and their colleagues in the Mediterranean world is that the message got its start among those who as Jews were already "conditioned" to "the mighty acts of God" or, as we would say today, already "softened up."

It will be readily granted that this is not generally the case of those outside the Church whom we would seek to win. But it cannot be said in honesty that it is more widely the case with those within the Church. The general secular worldview is the dominant influence among our own people, especially since it is not counteracted, as in former days, by regular Bible reading at home and family prayer. This is why, to anticipate liturgical matters to be discussed in the final chapter, I believe that we need Morning Prayer as well as Holy Communion at the service at which most of our people will be. Our worship is the only contact that most of our people have with the teaching of their religion all week; and we must over and over again set forth the whole "scheme." Before our people are ready for the Good News of Christ (in the Eucharistic lectionary) and for the re-enactment of the Atonement and the opportunity to re-enter therein (the main stress of the Eucharist in the Western rites), it is important to celebrate with our people the reality of God's presence in His world, of the fact of His providence, His involvement in history, His expectations for us, and His consequent judgment of us.

2. It is obvious that we simply can't preach the *kerygma* as "packaged" in the form we find these sermons in the New Testament; and we must keep in mind the fact that the Apostles did not preach just the words that are recorded on the pages of Scripture: we have the summaries and that's all. Obviously they filled out the message. And with what? One can reasonably assume that various elements of the *kerygma* were interpreted in terms of the problems and needs of their hearers and given application in terms of the actual situation of their own day. Since they were followers of a Lord who taught in parables and ministered in real action to real people, certainly we can assume that the apostolic preaching was "existential" in approach.

So too now in preaching the skeleton must be enfleshed. With what? Certainly not with traditional doctrinal phrases (as, for example, in the first sermon on the Holy Trinity previously referred to under the heading "The Concern of This Book," where traditional doctrinal concepts are simply mouthed—the communication simply being typical phrases repeated with gestures. A revival of biblical theology has certainly been a good thing in terms of our better understanding of the message; but its effect, in some quarters has been a biblicism in preaching which "touches ground" with the modern era no more than the "doctrinal" and conceptual preaching for which biblical theology was meant to be a corrective. A phrase like "saved by the blood of the lamb" offers no more to the average modern hearer than does "one substance with the Father." Sometimes among those attending church or now beginning again, people of fundamentalist background have a kind of nostalgia for the old phrases, and perhaps receive some spiritual inspiration from them, but, as far as understanding goes, they are merely holy noises; however, to the bulk of our hearers such preaching does not even have any discernable effect.

So the kerygmatic message in the New Testament gives us what the message is, but does not tell us how to preach it. But in telling us what the message is, it frees us to use whatever—and I mean whatever—provides the most effective means of communication. And we can use such with a clear conscience, and without a sense of heresy. The *kerygma* quite clearly marks out what is essential (and therefore gives the implication as to what is non-essential). It enables us to follow in our preaching Søren Kierkegaard's dictum that we should have an absolute relationship to the absolute and a relative relationship to all else.

If we were in a tradition which bound us to a specific theological or philosophical system—the relative having been absolutized, then we would have to abide by it in our preaching, in all loyalty. Since we are not so bound, Anglicans have no excuse for failure to communicate. And yet, our preaching has no special reputation, as compared with other Christian bodies, touching its effectiveness as to hearers. What has been standing in the way, considering an opportunity that would seem to be greater than that of those in other principal traditions? There are at least three such factors:

1. In our seminary courses and in most of our theological reading (assuming parsons who do continue to read) the content has been packaged in a way different from the thought-processes of the man in the street.

To preach in conventional terms takes no rethink-

ing on our part, no translation: in short, it's *easier*.
I will never forget the comment of a great theological professor at whose feet I was privileged to sit, and who was able to express to us the profundities of the faith both in Greek philosophical and in biblical language. One Monday morning he began his lecture with some heat, saying in effect, "I have just heard that some of you have been preaching what I say in here. Don't do that. You have got to translate it first." This was Paul Tillich speaking and it proved that he himself practiced what he preached: compare the difference in approach in his *Systematic Theology* and his *Shaking of the Foundations*—a collection of sermons.

This comparison is not meant to suggest that seminary instruction should consist of a series of homilies cast in molds suitable for preaching. If we did not use the conventional theological shorthand for instruction, we probably would have to extend the course to five years. And then the graduates would not be semantically equipped to read most of the centuries of theological literature.

And as a matter of fact, I have some sympathy with the person who is regularly preaching out of his seminary notes. The trouble is we have not yet a sufficiently developed sense of lay responsibility; our clergy are expected to do all sorts of things of which others could easily relieve them. This plus our short-handedness of "professionals" in the work of the Church, especially in expanding areas, means that insufficient time is left—or appears to be left—for the hard work involved in successful communication. Here again, the children of darkness are wiser in their generation than the children of light. The producer of a sponsored weekly network program generally makes it a full-time job merely to "get across" for half an hour. It takes a week's work. If this is true of communication as to passing worldly concerns, all the more would it seem to be true in regard to the communication of eternal verities. When a man has a full-time—or even over-time— job with all the other aspects of parish life and administration it is easy to see why many a preacher on Sunday morning resorts to the "relevant" cliché, on the one hand, or on the other, to undigested and untranslated theological analysis which has been pounded into his head during his theological education.

2. The very excellence of our liturgy provides a rationalization for inadequate thought and preparation as to the preaching. Some of a particular group within our Church sometimes put it boldly: "It's the Mass that matters." Many of us of varying emphases within the Church have, out of the goodness of our hearts, "covered" clergy in other parishes whose laymen criticize their preaching,

by saying, "The main thing you go to Church for is the service." And yet this is on the verge of heresy: our formularies keep the sacraments and the word in pretty careful balance (in fact, the Ordinal puts somewhat more emphasis—rightly or wrongly—on the word than it does on the sacraments). This difficulty is one that arises out of the truth of the situation: as we will see in Chapter IV, the liturgy *can* be a powerful adjunct to the preached word, indeed it is one way in which the Word can be preached. But it is unfortunate when this true fact gets turned around and becomes an excuse for ineffective use of the time set aside for preaching.

3. The Prayer Book can present another obstacle. Unless we take thought to the contrary, we tend to fall into Prayer Book phrases and words in our seeking to communicate religious ideas. It is an interesting fact that, although Episcopal clergy have little experience with extemporary prayer (compared with other Protestant brethren), the fact is that when they are called upon to perform in this manner, they generally turn out "smoother" prayers than those accustomed to this attempt. Why? Because our unconscious and conscious minds are well stocked with fine phrases from the book. This is fine in the realm of prayer. It is somewhat less helpful in the realm of preaching. We have all

heard sermons which consist largely of a rosary of phrases out of the Prayer Book. This is hardly preferable, as far as the art of communication is concerned, to a sermon strung together from biblical phrases, or one made up of a series of traditional doctrinal propositions.

Apparently there is little we can do (since our General Convention is not much interested in Prayer Book revision) about the difficulty of communication which the Prayer Book presents; but we are certainly free of General Convention when it comes to the terminology of our sermons; and it is too bad when Elizabethan English takes over here also. Sometime ago I invited a non-church-going (and perceptive) friend to attend a service on a Holy Day, and he heard a short sermon made up principally of phrases from the Collect, the Proper Preface for the Day and from the Ordinary of the Eucharist. I asked him how he liked the address. He said, "It was a nice ceremonial sermon—like the rest of the service." I pressed him as to just what he meant, and he added: "The preacher made the proper kind of noises for such an occasion." In other words, as to this intelligent visitor the sermon was simply another part of the service—perfectly orthodox and inoffensive, but all too quaint in its communication.

Now what are some of the ways we can communicate in our day? There are a number of ways. Each of us must work this out his own way in terms of the particular people he is dealing with and of the particular experience he has had, pastorally and otherwise. But I have selected two approaches for illustration.

1. For many people today the language of depth psychology is a better clothing for the Gospel than either Greek philosophy or Hebrew Messianic language. Modern psychological writings—both in professional works and in popular versions—start with personal problems, most of which can be grouped under the general heading of "anxiety." And what are the principal forms of anxiety which people recognize within themselves? I think that they are fear, guilt, inhibition, frustration, loneliness, indecision and despair. There may well be others, but I have not in my pastoral experience found any others which cannot be grouped under these headings. These are the main things which are bothering people.

It is true that these forms of anxiety raise penultimate questions: none of these, as such, touches the ultimate question of human existence. And it is true there is a danger that in addressing ourselves to penultimate questions we may get penultimate answers rather than the ultimate answers which we are commissioned to preach.

And yet, isn't it possible to give ultimate answers to penultimate questions? We can often start with a penultimate question and show that behind the penultimate question there is an ultimate question, and then give the ultimate answer. Our problem is to help our hearers see that the thing that is bothering them is really a deeper question than they themselves realize and thus see that the Christian answer is relevant and connected—and will take them further even than they may have wanted to go.

It's rather like having a decorator in, intending that he improve a particular room. If he's clever, he'll have arranged to do over the whole house before he leaves. Our problem is like the initial one of the interior decorator: how get into the house?

I will give one sermon as an example, as an indication of how without (I trust) any unfaithfulness to the Gospel, we can start where people are. Now, one of the most grievous problems of human personalities is *the reconciliation of self-criticism and self-acceptance*. How can one be really honest with oneself, avoiding rationalizations—and still live with oneself? A man needs self-acceptance or he can't live with himself; he needs self-criticism or others can't live with him. The two sound irreconcilable. People tend to think they can't have both; so they choose self-acceptance. And they achieve this by a process of rationalization and excuse-making. Now, homiletically one can address oneself to a problem like this. Granted, it is not the ultimate problem of life. But it's a problem people have. What do I do with my uneasiness about myself. Do I hide it? Do I face it? If I face it, how can I stand myself—how can I hold my head up and keep going? Jesus didn't mind addressing himself to some of these problems, which were short of final solutions. If a man needed healing, he needed healing. If he were hungry, he was to be fed.

There are blockages to the hearing of the Gospel. And here is one; if a man cannot hear the Law, he can't hear the Gospel, and he can't hear the Law if he is afraid that if he hears the Law, he won't be able to stand himself anymore. So I think the approach here is to analyze the way people do seek to sustain their sense of self-acceptance and dodge self-criticism.

So we can start with the process of rationalization. The source of guilt-feelings is the gap between the "is" and the "ought." Since the "is" generally falls short of the "ought," the usual practice is to pull the "ought" down to match the "is," so that we can feel comfortable with ourselves. "I'm as good as the next fellow." (I may not like the next fellow, but he is useful in this connection.) Or, "I'm a good fellow—I pay my taxes, mend my fences, don't kick my neighbor's dog, don't butt into other people's business, don't talk religion; I'm o.k." By using a set of mediocre ethics, we don't feel the need of redemption because we don't feel guilty. Or, it's someone else's fault: "I wouldn't have done what I did, if he hadn't done what he did!" Or, I'm a "dead-end kid!" Or, "My analyst tells me that because when I was twelve years old my mother glared at me, I had a traumatic experience: that's why I act the way I act." Or, some good came out of the evil: "I certainly gave her a piece of my mind, it will do her a wor-r-r-ld of good." Anything to make us feel all right with ourselves.

Then we can move to the results of such "cover-ups:"

1. They numb the sense of self-criticism. We stay in the same old moral ruts. We keep on year after year being offensive in precisely the same ways, until finally our friends write us off, saying, "Well, that's just the way he *is,* you know"—which means, he's a vegetable. The difference between a human being and an animal or vegetable is that a person doesn't have to stay the way he is. When one is written off as just being *the way he is,* then his humanity is being attacked—maybe he deserves it; that may be Judgment.

2. The second defect is, and here especially we can use the resources of modern depth psychology,

that by these rationalizations, we don't get rid of our sense of guilt: we simply put blankets on top of it and cause it to sink down into the subconscious where it makes us sick, in body as well as in soul—as we know from psychosomatic medicine.

Note the second chapter of Mark. A bed-ridden man, let's say an arthritic, is before our Lord. Jesus doesn't just say, like that, "Thy sins be forgiven thee." It's not that *ex opere operato*. He was the Good Shepherd, which means he was a good pastor, and as such he would not simply proclaim holy sentences at people. I can assume that again this is a *Reader's Digest* summary, and that He counselled with the man and found out what was really bothering him: what Mark quotes is the climax of the story. The man had a sense of guilt; Jesus freed him of that; then he said, "Get up and walk." Why not? It is so simple today, as we see psychosomatic connections, that the miraculous side of it is in danger. Thirty years ago we would have hesitated to preach on an event like that: the people would have found it incredible—so unscientific. Now, it's so scientific that we have difficulty in preserving the miracle in it! If you can help a bed-ridden man get rid of a deep sense of guilt, often he can get up and walk. It is as Jesus said, "Greater things you can do." Pastors—and psychoanalysts—today have helped people get free of a problem like that and they do get well. We *do* save the miraculous if we think about it more profoundly, because it's a very miraculous world in which spirit and flesh are so linked together: the whole thing is a *big miracle*. But the particular moment is not so amazingly miraculous. There is a connection between how we handle our guilt and how we feel physically and how we are able to function. Obviously this does not mean that everyone you know who is sick is therefore guilty. But it does mean that a man who is guilty and doesn't know how to handle it will be sick. You can be sure of that. He will be sick.

Now, the setting of the stage this way starts with something a person already recognizes as a problem. The answer to the problem is the Gospel. How do you avoid shoving a sense of guilt down into the unconscious, and how do you avoid carrying it around in the conscious mind? (If you carry it around in the conscious mind, you can't function either—you're hang-dog, no good to anybody; you feel inferior; you are ineffective.) What then do you do with it?

At this point in such a sermon I sometimes tell a story which I will tell now very briefly: We were moving into our summer house on Cape Cod about ten summers ago. We started out from New York in plenty of time to stock in all the food needed for the next day. But due to too many stops for four children for too many purposes we were late in getting there. But we did finally find a light in a little "general store" and succeeded in making purchases of what we needed for breakfast. I did have the wisdom to buy one of those three-cornered things for the kitchen sink. Well, by mid-morning that was full; and as I was going downtown to stock in anyway, I told my wife that I would buy a more adequate receptacle: I bought a step-on can. That was full by the next morning, and she then said, "Jim, you've got to get at this problem more basically"; so I took the back seat out of the station wagon and went into a hardware store in a larger town nearby and got a great big galvanized can— in fact two of them. That solved the problem for a week. Then what? You know how these modern houses are today—lots of closet space.

Here the congregation gets the point—and it's time to move back to the analogue, by some such statement as, "nor is it healthy to suppress guilt in the subconscious." But one shouldn't move on quite yet to the Gospel answer: the people are still wondering what happened in the analogy. Hence, after a pause: "You're probably wondering what we decided to do [they were]; well, we decided to arrange for an outside agency to take it off our hands."

Now, you see the congregation ready for the

Gospel. Right now is the time to affirm that the unique thing about the Christian faith is that we believe in a God who has the resources to take all the sin, all the hurt, yes all the filth of the world unto Himself. This is our central teaching. This is why in our iconography the central feature is the Cross—not the Golden Rule, not the Summary of the Law. I said once in a sermon that as to the moral universe God is the great Garbage Collector; and I offended a nice old lady who gave the Church $1,000 a year. I don't say that anymore. But I meant to say it: He is, you know.

The point is, in summary, you can't keep it around the conscious mind (the "kitchen" you simply *must* tidy up once in a while), and you don't dare lock it up in a closet. Who's to take it away? The "Lamb of God who takest away the sins of the world." God meets us where we are, not where we ought to be, takes the hurt out of our lives, accepts us even though we are not acceptable, thus enabling us to accept ourselves and have the courage to become like that which He has *taken* us to be, namely, acceptable.

The preacher can develop this further; for example, to avoid the "free ride" feeling ("Should we sin the more that grace abound?") He can indicate that the Christian is a man who accepts himself, though unacceptable, because God accepts him, and *therefore* in grateful response to that gift is an expert in taking up the hurts in the lives of other people. The Christian is the expert in meeting people as they are and not where they ought to be, of taking up the slack between himself and others, in accepting the unacceptable—or those he has deemed to be such.

If you've gotten this across, and it is understood and perceived, now is the time to give the copyright notice. There are preachers in our Church who are very good at explaining things in plain terms where people live, but who never mention any traditional names. I feel that I owe it to the great theological heritage, and to the people who have worked these things out under standard-brand labels, to attach the labels before I get through. Otherwise, they will say, "He just thought that up last night," or think that it was some special message of the Holy Ghost to him direct, when really we have nothing more than *the* Gospel—and our role is simply one of communication and translation. Therefore, I always say at the end of a sermon—take for example this one: "Now this is what the Church has always meant by *justification* (which doesn't mean being right, it means being taken for right) *by grace* (not earned, sheer gift) *through faith* (responding in repentance and in belief in the promises of a God who is everlastingly this way, whose very nature and property is to forgive and have mercy) *unto good works,* good works as the fruits of the free gift of salvation—not as the wages of salvation—(we had a reformation over that!).

The labels come in very well if people have understood up to this point that you have been talking about *them*. Now you can talk the language of traditional theology: justification, and sanctification as the fruit of justification.

I'm not saying this is a good sermon or that any other person ought to preach it. But it does demonstrate that it is possible to start with a problem that is less than the final problem of existence and still move to the *kerygma*, the old answer, the Gospel, at the end of the story.

Now, if one is doing a series and can approach another aspect of it, one will note that we've been on the human receiving-end. We've been talking in terms of man's justification. We haven't dealt with the more ultimate problem of God's Atonement—from His direction. One can address oneself to the first seven chapters of Romans, which deals not with the justification of man, but with the justification *of God*—meaning in short, "If God can deal with me, where have His standards gone! Where's His integrity, if He accepts *me*? After all, one is judged by the company one keeps. We *know* He forgives sins. How then can He be righteous?" This is a way of getting at the problem which we do not often use; but that's what St. Paul was most worried about. He was more worried about God than he was about man, at this point. He was trying to save God's reputation from being that of a "softie."

Now this is a question in which we can interest people, if we start in human terms. How can a wife meet a husband on his own level (when he has been renegade in one way or another) and give him the love and support and strength he needs— and at the same time not let down her standards? She mustn't act as though it doesn't matter what he does. Yet, if she stands on a pillar and says, "When you prove to me that you'll no longer be the way you've been, then you can come back," then he doesn't have the support and strength, i.e., the Grace, he needs to come back. He will find more comforting the distraction which caused the trouble —whether it be the bottle or an affair. And yet, if she says, "Everything is o.k. with me," she has really let him down, because she is really saying to him, "You don't matter either." The problem is how can she hold to her standards and still accept him— *now*, not when he proves that he is fit to come back. I think we all know the answer. She has to take into herself the hurt of the situation. Even on the human level the biblical word is true: *Without the shedding of blood, there is no remission of sins.* There is no way of reconciling human beings, where there is a barrier, unless some one takes up the hurt of the matter. Well, in some such mysterious way, this is true in the heart of God. For Him to be absolutely pure in His standards—in other words, to have the greatest expectations of us—is the source of our human dignity. Judgment is good news too: it means that *God cares what I do!* The Ultimate Ground of the Universe cares what I do—that makes me important. I am significant, because God judges me. If He did not, then the only answer to life is a "So what?"

The saddest thing in the world is to screw up your courage and go to someone and tell him you are sorry, only to have him say, "Oh, skip it! I don't care what you do!" This is really terrible; it makes clear you're so unimportant to him that you can't even hurt him. The capacity to be hurt by a given person is a reflection of his significance to the person who can be so hurt. The point is, God does not say "skip it." When we say this we get into all kinds of theological paradoxes as to His passivity and imperturbability. But the Cross shows that in one part of the nature of His being, He can be hurt; He does care what we do; and He takes up the hurt. If the person to whom you go to apologize says, "What you did bothered me a great deal, but I'm glad we've gotten back together again," this shows you count. This is redemptive; saying "Skip it" is not. The Atonement in some mysterious way is *how* He takes it.

Here you may wish to explain one or more of the classical theories of the Atonement; but, if you do, it is important to say that the Church has never officially adopted any one of these theories. Just as in the case of the Real Presence we affirm the fact and the reality and are not tied to any particular theory as to mechanics (whether transubstantiation, consubstantiation, receptionism, virtualism, or what not), so here we affirm the *fact* of the Atonement (i.e., the dogma) and we do not insist on any particular *doctrine* of the Atonement. Indeed here we are dealing with one of the most profound mysteries touching the very heart of God—one which we cannot probe too deeply. But as to the reality of it we have the evidence not only of the words of our Lord and the whole biblical teaching about the nature of God ("whose nature and property is ever to have mercy and to forgive") but also the experience of millions of people who through their belief in the Cross have had their lives changed.

Again, if one were preaching a series in this general area it would be well to turn somewhat more particularly to the matter of *sanctification* as the fruit of justification (of course, not starting with such a formidable label). This particular sermon in the series would pick up with how God is to us in His justifying action through the Atonement, reminding the congregation that the natural response to such a great Gift is *thanksgiving*.

How does God want us to express this thanksgiving? In prayer and praise, of course. But actually He needs nothing of us—and our fellow creatures *do*. His attitude can be likened to that of the man who wisely makes provision that at his death the funeral notice shall read "Please omit flowers; contributions may go to" his favorite charity. The way God wants us to express our thankfulness is *to repeat the act*. He has met us where we are; He wants us to meet others where they are. He has taken the hurt out of our lives, He wants us busy taking the hurt out of other people's lives. He has accepted the unacceptable; He wants us to do the same thing. This is the meaning of the word in the first Epistle of John: *Beloved, if God so loved us, we ought also to love one another*.

Then at this point we should remind our hearers that this does not mean that our status with God is established or gained by these good works; rather they are the thankful fruit of a status already freely conferred. Here I have found a helpful illustration out of my experience of visiting a pineapple factory in Hawaii. The various machines were producing various kinds of results—slices, chunks, juice, sticks (for "Old Fashioneds"), hulls (for cattle fodder), etc.—except one machine which was running, but from which nothing came out. I asked the attendant why, and he answered, "Because no pineapples are going in the other end." While works are not the means of justification, if the works are not happening we can well doubt that justification has occurred; for example, whether if in true repentance there has been the faith that makes us meet for the Grace.

It can be pointed out again that our clue as to the principal kind of goodness expected of us is the way that God is good to us. God's love for us is *agapé*; our love for our brethren should be *agapé*. This is, of course, the kind of love specified in the Greek original of the text from the first Epistle of John.

Now, this third sermon suggested does not start precisely with a felt human need; but it need not if it is simply a completion of the first sermon by way of the third in the series. But if it is to stand as a sermon on its own it should perhaps bear some such title as "Why be Good?" and the first five minutes should probably consider the question people raise in their minds about being good to others: "What's the point?—they don't appreciate it!" "What's he ever done for me?", etc. Here we touch ground. And in developing the sermon as suggested above we can stress the point that we should be good to others not because they are good to us, but because *God* is good to us. We should forgive others not because they forgive us but because God has forgiven us. We should accept others not because they have accepted us but because God has accepted us.

All the above stems out of an approach to the anxiety arising from a sense of one's guilt. Actually the other aspects of human anxiety can be treated in this general way. My conviction is that each of the distinguishable forms of anxiety finds its answer in basic Christian belief. Our task is to make the connection. I will not seek here fully to develop the import of these anxiety states and the connection with the various teachings of the Faith, since I have done this in *Beyond Anxiety**; but here, with the exception of guilt more fully discussed above, I summarize the connections simply in order to reinforce my main point.

Fear. Fear has it real roots in idolatry (either monolatrous—one false god, or polytheistic—several). Something less than God has become an ultimate basis of reliance or focus of interest, and, consciously or unconsciously, the feet of clay have been perceived. The answer to fear then is a thoroughgoing monotheism, a confidence that we can safely put all our eggs in one basket, if it's the right

* Scribners (1953).

basket. The answer is in all simplicity: *Hear, O Israel, the Lord thy God is one.*

Inhibition. Many of our people, due to general cultural conditioning (Puritanism and Pietism, which made a great mark in our culture, as has to a lesser degree the world-denying strain in Roman Catholicism) have been considerably crippled in their ability really to enjoy, in its physical aspects, the kind of world God has made. The secret to freeing our people in this regard is a sound Doctrine of Creation. *On the sixth day the Lord looked down on all that he had made and said, It is very good.* If the world is good enough for God to have made, it is good enough for us to enjoy. Actually in the Judeo-Christian tradition Judaism and Anglicanism are the heritages remaining most free from the joy-crippling heresy which is largely responsible for the widespread sense of inhibition in people's conscious and unconscious minds. In this connection you should take occasion to explain the sacramental character of the sexual relationship in marriage (you may want to point out that even our Church, in this country, has yielded somewhat to the general Protestant atmosphere, as is indicated by the omission from our Marriage Office of the words [in the English Prayer Book] from the groom to the bride: "With my body I thee worship.").

Frustration. Just as the Cross is the answer to

guilt, it is, seen in another light, the answer to frustration. Here we have to point out that limitation need not be frustration. Every person is limited in one way or another; if limitation is frustration then everyone is doomed to frustration. The significant thing about self-fulfillment is what we do *within* our limitations. One of the best illustrations I know is the life of the Rt. Rev. Samuel Isaac Schereschewsky, Bishop of Shanghai (now about to be canonized at the second passing of the "minor Holy Days" at the forthcoming Episcopal General convention—his saint's day is October 15.* Then from that we move to his inspiration—and ours: Christ on Calvary. Only three hours (tradition says); but more for the weal of more people through these three hours than any other period of time in any man's life anywhere. Each of the "Seven Words" can be pointed to this end; concern for His persecutors ("Father, forgive them . . ."); concern for His fellow-victim of capital punishment ("this day . . ."); concern for His family responsibilities ("Mother, behold thy son" and *vice versa*); concern—and a proper one—for himself ("I thirst"); the great proclamation of faith as to the meaningfulness of it all. (*Eloi, eloi lama sabacthani*," in which He "filed by title" the whole of Psalm 22); the ultimate

* *See Apostle of China,* by James Mueller.

words of trust ("Father, into thy hands . . ."); and the final words of victory ("It is finished") is finished for Him—and for *us*. It is not the broad, lazy river that makes the power; it is the narrow stream through the gorge.

Indecision. After a description of the process of decision-making, one can move to problems of human fallibility, the importance of total action *now,* God's claim on us now so to act.* The dimension of trust which all this involves—including trust that God can always help us bring good out of what turns out to be wrong—leads to the most profound aspects of God's Providence and of the nature of faith.

Loneliness. Why are people lonely, even in crowds? People yearn for deep, abiding relationships. This leads us quite easily into one important aspect of the doctrine of the Holy Spirit, the source of the Holy Community, the peace of deep and abiding relationships. You can see what I have said on this in *Beyond Anxiety,* but I hope you do better with it than I did, since this is one topic on which I don't feel I have really ever "rung the bell." Here lonely people (especially those who have known intimate relationships, such as widows and divorcees) need more talk than about the Holy Ghost.

* See here the superb statement by Professor Søe quoted in my *Doing the Truth* (Doubleday), pp. 97 f.

In part, the answer is that we would give under the rubric of "frustration;" in part it is actual pastoral help in the ways of "meeting people," etc. (through parish groups and otherwise).

Despair. Here, if we analyze aright, the real nature, psychologically and otherwise, of human restlessness and meaninglessness, we are set to lead straight into the doctrine of eternal life: the affirmation of the permanence of all that we do in God's whole grand plan and the significance of the *now* for the *forever. We* must meet the bifurcation often made between life now and life to come by affirming the continuity of the whole thing, and the equal importance of all that is now and all that shall be.

These are not sermon outlines; they are simply suggestions as to how we may relate pressing personal problems with the eternal truth.

But anxiety problems are not the only way in, as I have suggested before. There are several other important avenues. Another is the use of one or another of real social concerns.

As in the case of anxiety problems—where we deal with them in order to help people with these very problems, but also see in these problems an avenue to the preaching of the Gospel, so in the case of social concerns we are exercising the responsibility of prophecy, but at the same time are utilizing an avenue for explaining to people the eternal meaning of things. Now this is not a book on meeting people's anxieties, nor on "the social gospel." Here our interest is how these avenues can serve the communication of the Gospel. In this context, given a contemporary and public—"newspaper"—event as a starting point, the listener in the pews knows what it is, or if he has failed to read the paper, he can through you—the preacher—very quickly be brought to realize that there is an important problem to be understood and interpreted.

There are several precise conditions for the "public affairs" type of preaching. They are, among others:

1. Get the story straight. Don't use current news as a "tee" unless you have that news straight.

2. Explain the facts clearly. Some of the congregation may not have read the paper carefully, or may not have grasped the importance of the particular event or issue.

3. But don't get too bogged down in the event itself and the practical factors connected with it, either in terms of analysis or solution. We can contribute to our society, *en passant,* in this regard (and this is fulfilling our prophetic role), but we should do so with a fairly "light touch," since our

main purpose is to preach the Gospel. If analysis of the situation to which we are addressing ourselves requires ten minutes, then it may mean that the sermon has to be thirty minutes (in spite of the general assumption that the limit is twenty minutes). By no means take eighteen minutes analyzing the current news, leaving only two minutes for what in so short a time is bound to be a cliché, rather than the Gospel. If, this is the proportion of things, there is a real danger that all that we will have said in the seat of God's Word is "Up and at 'em!" or "Do something" or "Pray about this." This is a misuse of the pulpit.

4. Don't worry about infallibility. By this I mean don't be silent for fear that you might not be proven to be right in your judgment on the situation. First of all, in reading your Bible and thinking in terms of the whole perspective on things, you are pretty apt to recognize evil when you see it, and be able to debunk those who make evil look like good. But even if, these considerations in mind, you are proven to be wrong, remember that your main task is to stir *concern*, not provide precisely correct answers. To use an old aphorism (which I am always surprised to find has not been too widely circulated), the purpose of preaching is to comfort the afflicted and to afflict the comfortable. If your sermon does this latter, you are helping your people

face a current problem and seek right answers, even if yours may not be the one which finally recommends itself it them.

5. Deal with issues, but do not align with parties or personalities. If you do, you may find that half your congregation will not "hear" you when you next talk about an issue.

6. Don't use this approach too frequently. You may find that you have to "sit out" certain issues, simply because you have said a good deal already about other public matters (I need refer only to the "Wolf, wolf" story). If last Sunday you made a big noise about some controversial question (with the resulting irritation of a portion of your congregation and of others in the community) then by all means the next Sunday talk about Prayer, or the meaning of the Liturgy. (I do not say this cynically: these latter things are important things to talk about, in any case.) In all this there is a need for a certain "staging" of things.

Just as in the case of preaching on anxiety problems, there is always a danger that, in dealing with public matters, we will give answers only on the same level as the questions. This is neither being true to our prophetic task nor is it the preaching of the Gospel. Our contemplation of the current scene should force us back to the Bible and its deeper meanings.

I will give an example that was rather current when these words were first spoken, but which now has taken a somewhat different shape. You will remember that in the same month Russia had launched Sputnik a comparative survey of the educational systems of the U.S.S.R. and the U.S. showed that we are behind in many vital matters; hence an inferiority complex (quite useful at times) was spreading among our people.

Turn to the Epistle for the 21st Sunday after Trinity (Eph. 6:10 ff.). Here, through the aid of Dr. Rudolf Bultmann, we realize that Paul was speaking in terms of an astrological world-view: in common with most people of his time, he really believed that there were spheres in the heavens, which dominated our lives here. At the time Bultmann pointed this out, he was quite right on the point and Paul was wrong, and his view was sound that in interpreting the passage we must "de-mythologize" it. But oddly enough, through our human science, we have made St. Paul right; for the first time since he wrote the passage it is true! Namely, those spheres are up there; we put them there. And these spheres do dominate our lives. They affect our Government spending, our tax-ation, our design for a pragmatic educational pro-gram to meet the challenge, even threaten the depreciation of our accustomed freedoms. The preacher can affirm that St. Paul's κοσμοκράτορες are realities. Then we can turn with relevance to the projected solution. Though our freedom is limited by these things, we can make a "breakthrough" to the God that is above all of these things. In our exposition we can structure our sermon around each of St. Paul's examples from pieces of the armor worn by soldiers in his day. Just one example: "Having your loins girt about with truth": honesty about the U-2 plane and the Russian crisis, as events proved, would have been better than an elaborate lie. "Having on the breastplate of righteousness:" if we were not prepared to back up the Hungarian revolutionaries, why did we condition them for freedom through Voice of America and Radio Free Europe? Why did we block Israel in Egypt in the Sinai Peninsula and in the same week do nothing about Russia in Hungary? "Your feet shod with the preparation of the Gospel of peace:" in spite of the insults of Mr. Khrushchev, at the very top of everything we do in the U.N. and the negotiation with the U.S.S.R. must be a constant presentation of a program of nuclear disarmament *cum inspection*.

Obviously, the force of such illustrations will vary as the news develops, and I am quite sure that by the time this book is out these comments will be less relevant than others which a given preacher can make. But the main point remains the same. We need not be "cabined in" by earthly forces less than ourselves, which are the works of our own hands, and which end up tending to dominate the makers thereof. God is above all and we can have a personal break-through direct to Him and thus retain our essential freedom and from His perspective bring judgment on what is going on, and from Him receive grace to help us redeem the time.

One more illustration of how we can take the current scene, move to the Bible, and then move back to the current scene. There is no question but that our public image has been damaged abroad. In trying to alert the country to this danger, it would be well for us to begin a critique of Communism (a view reassuring to the "right wing" of the congregation, which doubtless would include some of the Vestry). What are the four things we dislike most about Communism? (1) Materialism; (2) an "elite" group under which are subordinated others in the population; (3) religious discrimination; (4) denial of civil rights. Then turn to the story of David, Bathsheba and Nathan, with the text: *And Nathan said to David, Thou art the man.* It would be superfluous for me to outline what can be said about the U.S. in regard to these four points. By the time this book has reached you, what you can say will be worse or better—but different.

CHAPTER III

THE SALESMAN

Some years ago I was invited by a publishing firm to a sales conference in order to tell the assembled salesmen about a book of mine it was about to publish. In about half an hour I gave what was in effect a book review and then answered questions. Considering the fact that this was a book in the theological field, I was surprised at the high degree of concentration during my remarks and at the penetrating questions I was asked. Afterwards I said to the religious editor that either their salesmen were particularly religious in their interests or that I must have been in particularly good form. "Neither is necessarily the case," he said candidly. "They want to sell books." He went on to say that a comparable degree of concentration might well accompany authors' reviews of a book on anything from child care to gerontology. And before I was "put on," I heard the end of a lecture by the sales manager on methods of approaching and "stating the case," whatever the book, to bookstore owners and buyers.

The analogy is too obvious to labor. The old saw

63

about the "better mousetrap" has a measure of truth in it; but successful businesses don't rely on it. They know that sales depend on more than a reasonably good product and attractive packaging: almost equally important is the effectiveness of the salesman. And his effectiveness depends in good measure both on his approach and on his preparation for the task.

What does the preacher do by way of preparation to support his hope that in his own ministry and in his own peculiar way, following no one else's bent, he may "sell" the Gospel? Now, as we all know Phillips Brooks said, preaching is truth mediated through personality; hence there is no universal pattern. That's why there's no use trying to read somebody else's sermon out of a book. I am sure some of you have tried that in desperation—and have learned it doesn't make a very good sermon. It doesn't even sound good to you—let alone to those who are listening, because we are all so different as "mediators"—and we ought to be. To return to the sales conference referred to above, I asked my host why they didn't save a lot of time by simply supplying the salesman with a brief squib about each book and let them say that to the buyers. He answered, "We do that too; but we want the salesman really to grasp the purport and drift of a book and then to tell the buyer about it in his own way —and in the way the particular buyer will 'get it'."

What is it that we should do to enable us to understand the people to whom we are preaching, understand our message, and then translate the message in terms of the concepts and needs—real or apparent—of those to whom we are preaching?

Now first I will say some very obvious things, simply filing them by title. Of course, one needs a sense of vocation, a sense of dedication, and the practice of daily prayer and worship. These are things which can make any Christian do his job better; they are not special things for the priest. These are things for lawyers who would try to be Christian lawyers, and physicians who would be Christian physicians, and businessmen who would be Christian businessmen. The "practice of the presence of God" and activity and decision-making "under judgment" are not uniquely appropriate to the priesthood; they are appropriate for every Christian in the exercise of his vocation and ministry.

So we turn to the special things the preacher should do. At the outset, I'll admit that I do not very much believe in preparation for a particular sermon. What is needed is a continuing body of preparation to relate the Word to the situation. Our reading should not be limited to stuffing ourselves on Saturday night with various commentaries, collections of illustrative stories (aren't most of such books dreadful?), religious poems, etc.

Then how get ready? First, the preacher should

continue his theological study and his study of the Bible and commentaries thereon consistently right through so that he is developing a reservoir of ideas as to biblical material to use (rather than for each sermon trying to locate biblical material to decorate his own passing ideas). In this connection the discipline of the Daily Office can be most helpful. I am not ignoring its devotional value; but here I'm talking about the pedagogic value for the preacher. Since Morning and Evening Prayer provide, in course, the most telling passages of Scripture and coverage of most of the Psalms, they are a continual preparation for what the preacher should say. And this is true likewise of the fixed portions of the office. One constantly finds new light in the *Magnificat*, the *Nunc dimittis*, the *Venite* and the *Te Deum* and *Benedictus* and so forth, either because of the light thrown on them by the different psalms and lessons or because of one's own situation and problems at the time. The Church has been very wise in what it has selected as permanent material in these Offices because of its capacity to reflect the light of that material which changes. Hence, this is a very fine program of regular Bible reading. And there is nothing undevotional in being a little professional when you see a pretty good text or passage (one you perhaps haven't thought about since seminary—even if then) and tick it along the margin. After a considerable number of years of acquaintance with the Bible, I still find passages almost every other day that I didn't seem to have heard of before, or if I had, they hadn't "hit" me in the same way. That's one reason for continuing the Offices year after year: you're changing, the world's changing, you are dealing with different people than you dealt with before and things are going to have different meanings for you.

Second, the reading of commentaries and other theological books should always be done with a pencil so that you are keeping some permanent record of things to which to look back when you need material on a given subject. You cannot, in preparation for a particular topic, go through your whole library to find relevant things you need. You should be accumulating your material as you go— for any number of sermons.

Third, it is very important that you not limit your reading to religion. This would seem to contradict the charge in the Ordination of Priests: "Ye ought to forsake and set aside, as much as ye may, all worldly cares and studies, laying aside the study of the world and the flesh." But one can rightly interpret that to say that a picturization of the real problems of peoples' individual lives, the description of real social situations (see Chapter II), even written by a blatant secularist, often is really religious reading. And the same is true of the theater. It's a very good exercise to go to a play written by someone who perhaps has very little theological know-how and yourself analyze out of the raw data which is there what the theological issues are and what the theological answers are.

Now, in our secular reading—or plays or movie-going—we should be sanctifying the secular in that we are looking at the material from another perspective. More is involved than looking for sermon illustration or a witty line from the play (though that's not a bad idea either—and it's nice to look *au courant*). Rather, these activities help you to connect your knowledge of the Faith, your own personal experience and your vicarious pastoral experience, with various deep needs of the human spirit and in human relationships. Therefore, a certain range of reading beyond the strictly theological—novels, plays, non-fiction books—are very important if we are to be relevant preachers or parsons. Think of the meaning of the word *parson*. It is a corruption of the word "person." There were times in the history of our Church when the clergyman in the town was *the person,* i.e., he was the man who knew about things. He had had an education. He read books. He had books. All this in contrast to almost everyone else in the community. While these days with widespread higher education

we can no longer claim in many of our communities
to be "the persons," in a certain sense the word
"parson" should suggest to us that we should be
men of some breadth of culture quite beyond the
strictly theological.

At the same time, we need to be familiar with
such material so that we'll know what to talk about
and how to say it.

Fourth, out of our wide experience and contact
with people—that's one of the blessed things about
the ministry—we have a wide range open to us.
We have hundreds of homes and mothers and
fathers and brothers and sisters and lands: that
text is literally fulfilled. But out of all this we
should constantly be reacting in terms of what is
needed for people generally—distilling this out of
what we have experienced in the particular. This
doesn't mean that we share the secrets of the con-
fessional or for that matter that we talk about people's problems even when they are not within that
explicit limitation. Nevertheless, the particular
suggests the general and we ought to be filing away
ideas which will again be real as we preach, will
again start where somebody is likely to feel that it
matters.

Then how do we get together the particular sermon? What is the "drill" for that? I will say what
I think works best. There will be others who will

very much disagree and I am quite open to that because different people work differently.

It's a very good idea to know precisely what you are going to talk about the following Sunday at least by Tuesday. Now fortunately we have a discipline like that imposed upon us in many communities because that's about when the copy for the Saturday advertisement has to go in. I believe in heralded topics, first, because it does increase the attendance, and second, because it's a test of the preacher: if he cannot find a way to put in one line a question that someone will want to come and hear the answer to, then it's probably not a good sermon anyway. So by Tuesday we are forming a question. I always look at the lessons and at the Epistle and Gospel before I do this. The question selected, I keep thinking about that question from Tuesday on. (If my thinking about it leads me to think I am off the track and I really haven't got much to say on that topic, well, there's a last chance on the proofs for the ad.) Anyway, during this time I keep thinking about it, my own preparation is rather haphazard. In an odd moment I will go to a commentary and check something, or something occurs to me as another text that I might work into the whole and I go and look at that. I remember something I read in this book or that and I look at it. This is all in the course of every other thing going on during the week. And then Saturday evening I begin to pull it together and be sure I have seen all the material in the commentaries—at least on the bibical passage—and that I have gotten a kind of outline in my mind. Then I go to bed. I think it through once before going to sleep; and Sunday morning when I wake up I think it through again.

In my own case (and many other clergymen have told me that this often happens to them) a remarkable thing has occurred. The unconscious mind does go to work during the night; the dough put in the oven before going to bed will turn out to be pretty good biscuits in the morning. The sermon has become quite well organized. And having gone through it in my mind in the morning, I do not think about it again—until the service. Then I listen intently to the psalms and lections (I had looked at them before, but new light often comes for the sermon when they are set in the context of the actual worship of God and are not merely read in a study.) And then I go down to the pulpit and preach. Occasionally I have a note if there is a quotation I want to use (but I am not much for quotations, as indicated in the first chapter).

Now there are those who say that all this is very risky and that a young man should write out his sermons for five years and then later preach extemporaneously. But if he writes them out for five years, then he has accumulated such a "cracker barrel" that he'll never want to let go of it; and, with the high mobility of clergy these days, it's very easy to keep using the same stuff. You can use all this somewhere for three years and then you start all over again. My own feeling is the reverse. I think that a man should make a desperate attempt to preach extemporaneously. Many clergy just assume they can't. I'd rather have them stumble for a year, and perhaps finally they can do it. But if they really find they can't, all right; *then* is the time to start writing things out. There are some who simply cannot do it; but there are many who think they cannot who can. It's perfectly clear that there will not be quite the full elegance of English; there will be many dangling participles and a tape-recording of yourself is dreadful. But remember the people are themselves in an oral situation when the sermon is preached. They are not judging it in terms of grammatical structure. If you are going to publish later you are going to have to do a lot of work to smooth it out; but if you are just talking right then and there, the congregation doesn't notice how bad it is in structure. What they do notice is that *you're looking right at them*. And this has a great bearing on how you put things. It means that if they are looking blankly at you when you thought you had made an obvious point, you will use another illustration, you will develop it further. It means, too, that when they quickly react to something on which you were going to spend five minutes, you move on; they've got it: you don't waste their time and yours. You can see precisely where your people are.

It's this direct response *as you go* that counts. If they don't get it, you'd better stay on the point until they do. There's no use moving to Point 2 when they haven't grasped Point 1. On the other hand, if they have understood Point 1 before you have finished it, you had better move on to 2 quickly or they will start yawning. And the amazing thing is that if you try this and gain the courage to continue it, you often think of things right in the direct contact with the people that you would never have thought of even if you had prepared the sermon for four months. There is something about the *I-thou*, direct person-to-person relationship that opens a channel for the inspiration of the Holy Ghost. Who is the Holy Ghost? He is *saint esprit de corps*. He is the light and warmth of God working in the fellowship, and thus can inspire right directly from the fellowship.

Also one talks differently when one talks orally than he does when he has written something out. I once asked a professor at Columbia who is interested in semantics to make a check of various chapters of a book I had written. He took six sample chapters and I indicated which ones I had dictated in a recording machine and then polished up and which ones I had written out longhand. Now the ones dictated read pretty badly in typescript; I had to upgrade them considerably. The ones which had been written out longhand I had to try to downgrade in the interest of communication. I knew, before this professor reported, that it is much easier to upgrade rough material and still keep it fresh than to downgrade carefully written out material which is smooth. The professor's check showed this: in the material written out longhand, there were about twice as many Latin derivatives as compared with Anglo-Saxon derivatives. Now what most effectively communicates to people? Anglo-Saxon derivatives.

And here we should follow the spirit of the Incarnation. We must "stoop to conquer." I regret very much the general fall in cultural level. It is too bad that people are no longer interested in trying to comprehend much of the magnificent literary form that used to be characteristic of great preaching. As I look back at great sermons of past times, I admire their literary elegance, their balanced phrases, their allusions to all branches of literature including the Latin and Greek poets, their subtle suggestions relating to the Bible—where a whole train of thought could be set off by one allusion. Well, it's too bad; but few of our hearers have read those Latin and Greek poets any more, not many have read the Bible, the people listening to us haven't the remotest idea what we are talking about when we make these references.

Hence we must face the question: Who are we doing this for? Just for our own literary achievement? Or that we might save some man? And this leads me to the dual function of a Catholic Church. A sectarian Church, a Church that does not regard itself as having a visible continuity (flesh around its bones of theology) can quite well regard its task as simply providing the Gospel —simply laying before people the rudiments, the elements of the Gospel. But we claim to be a Church with a culture, an enfleshed theology. We have an art, a literature, a poetry, a music, a whole historical continual fabric; therefore we have a double job. We have the job of reaching people where they are with that which is saving, and then once we have attracted them—and stirred them, then our job is to elevate them into the whole culture. But as to the priorities, the first is more important: to reach them *at all*. And we must become simple—become even crude or even slangy or blunt or rough—to get at them where they are and then hope that having found them we can take them into the wholeness of this rich enfleshed system of life and thought.

This is the Incarnation. God was not above being translated into the language of a human life in a manger, and we should not be above descending to the level of comprehension, the level of interest, the level of concern, of those people we would reach. I am not saying this in a snobbish way. Our people have passed us up in many ways; in technological excellence, business know-how, they are oftener smarter than we are. But there has been a collapse in the classics, in the humanities, in the various things on which we have relied to make elegant sermons understood. So our first job is not elegance. Our first job is bringing with conviction the Gospel to people. Then if those we have so nourished can be brought into the whole heritage, appreciate anew the humanities which the Church has nurtured, well and good. If this were a book on Christian Education in the parish, I would like to say much about what we ought to be doing with our already "sold" adults. I am convinced that we have the task not only of bringing them a mature view of the theology and the ethic and so forth; I think we've got to teach the humanities in our Churches if we are to have persons who appreciate the wholeness of God's creation and the goodness and beauty of human life at its best levels, because these things are not being done in the public schools very much any more, and they are being done less and less even in colleges. Perhaps it may again be our task, as it was in the Middle Ages, to *educate* in the hope that there may be more whole people.

But, as I have said, all this is a secondary aim to the aim of reaching people at all. Therefore, I sum this up by saying it is better for us to preach less elegantly and more directly. But I would not want anyone to think that this means that we can thus be even busier in parish administration, pastoral calling, and various other distractions of the week and needn't prepare our sermons. This system if really done aright (and I don't claim that I have always so budgeted my time), involves more time, not less. It means really keeping your preaching on your mind all week as you go about other duties. It means really spending time reading the Bible, loyally participating in the Choir Offices, reading serious books about not only theology but other things, and even when you're at your leisure, such as the theater with friends, having a theological frame of mind as you are looking at the material—scouting always for material, for ideas and for your own deepening in these things. So it is not a question of less preparation; it's a question of *total* preparation *all* the time, which then expresses itself on each Sunday in a fresh way.

How learn the art? By doing it. To be more specific:

1. In the stage of your novitiate arrange to give as many addresses as possible in your parish —organize adult classes, arrange to give content talks at organization meetings, etc. All this is a good idea anyway; but in any case this out-of-pulpit activity "loosens up" the parson for talking without notes in Church.

2. Again in the stage of your novitiate (important limitation here: if you turn out to be good at it, you can accept but a percentage of the invitations) accept chances to speak elsewhere— in or out of the pulpit. You're usually more daring in someone else's pulpit: if you "muff it," you're leaving for your home town after the service anyway; and with the courage this affords you, you'll probably *not* muff it.

3. But the best way is an active program of *pastoral counselling*. Two things happen in this aspect of our ministry. Of course you want to help a given person with his given problem. Whether it's a problem of not being able to get along with the landlord all the way up to a question of keep-

ing a marriage pulled together or a question of faith in Christ, you want to help him for his own sake. He is not just a guinea pig.

But second, as you are explaining—and I don't believe in totally nondirective counselling—the structure and answers (either in the realm of moral theology or the realms of faith), and relating this to the particular problem and in relevant communication, you are getting fine practice in extemporaneous speech.

If someone comes to you who is a Jew who says he likes the Church and its liturgy, he likes the stands the Church has taken on important social issues—in short he'd like to come along with us; but he can't possibly grasp this idea of a Divine human being, then what you tell him for the next three-quarters of an hour in a way he can understand it—where he stands—is marvelous preparation for the kind of direct preaching that you ought to be doing. When a woman says that she is forty and she doesn't think she's got a chance of getting married and she's lonely, what you tell her sincerely and directly face to face is the best possible preparation for a sermon on that subject. And then there is the explanation of specific doctrines to people such as the difficult one, "Why did God have to have Jesus die on the Cross?" If you work *that* through with an individual, you are going to be better prepared to find words to say it than sitting down Saturday night with all the textbooks on the Atonement and trying to work out a scholarly outline about the subject. The same with the oft-restated Problem of Evil.

Therefore, the most important thing I would add to digesting the material and keeping in touch with current things that are not labeled religious and keeping the topic on one's mind throughout the week, is a continuous pastoral relationship with a wide variety of people, so that what you're saying you know is real and you know rings bells and you know hooks in where people are, because you've already tried it. It's already happened. It isn't just a theory any more.

Obviously one cannot in one twenty minute sermon cover the wholeness of the Gospel at any one time. But if one through his reading of the Bible, his contemplation, his prayer and his meditation, his sacramental life, his pastoral experience and his experience with life beyond the narrow borders of theology is keeping these things very close to his mind and heart, he will find that the Church itself—and its liturgy—tend to sort out the material for him. So all this will find its place sooner or later in one's preaching, and one's sermons will display contact with real experience and will be expressed in a relevant and understandable way.

CHAPTER IV

THE STORE

THE GOOD merchandiser relies on more than a sound product, attractive packaging and well-briefed salesmen. He counts on the store itself as a medium of sales. Take Christmas-time (which for merchandisers starts well before Thanksgiving). The goods are there for sale; but there's much more: an elaborate Christmas decor, carols piped over the loud-speaking system, a well-padded Santa Claus. None of this is directly for sale; but is meant to "condition" the purchasers to "get in the mood"; it softens them up for sales.

So too in the communication of the Gospel, the context—the service of worship—is important. The analogy is imperfect, of course, and for this important reason: Worship, whatever its form, is more than "window-dressing" or "atmosphere-creation." It has its own validity, quite apart from its contribution to—or distraction from—the preaching of the word. It would be significant if no sermon were ever preached. Such a situation would result in a vitamin-deficiency in the believers' spiritual diet; but what happens in worship, *happens*—and is real. If one were to assert that the

service is meant simply as an aid to the preaching
(and there is a strain in Protestantism which so
exalts the word that even the Lord's Supper is seen
only as a means of its proclamation), I would
say, rather, that the preaching is meant to be an
aid to worship, since worship of God is man's ultimate end, from which right thinking and right
acting are corollary. But here we are talking about
the communication of the Word; and the fact is
that the service—and its externals—can be a
means of communication. It can itself be a mode
of preaching. And it can provide a persuasive context for the preaching—like an attractive store for
the work of the salesman in "selling" the good
product well-packaged. Therefore it is without
any denigration of the primary role of the service
—worship for worship's sake, that we turn to its
principal *instrumental* purpose: aid toward the
preaching of the Gospel. If something is meant to
be a means to an end, a proper concern is: *How
well adapted is the means to the end?* And in
answering this question we can—and should be
—completely pragmatic. In evaluating our forms
and ceremonies the question is not what's right,
in some eternal sense; but what communicates?

Too often in discussions of the "proper" form
of the service—on the part of professionals as well
as of amateurs, the explicit or implicit norm of

judgment is an attempted eternalization of the temporal. "The Church has always . . ." (referring to a custom which originated in Italy in the nineteenth century); "It's Catholic to . . ." (do what Fr. So-and-So experimented with while the spokesman was an acolyte there); "It's wrong to . . ." (do anything more than the Rev. Mr. Such-and-Such did in old Christ Church). For some the norm is Adrian Fortescue's *Ceremonies of the Roman Mass Explained*; for some it is the "Sarum rite," as pieced together from Percy Dearmer's *Parson's Handbook*, the publications of the Alcuin Club and the *Chichester Customary*; for some it is how he remembers thing were done—or *not* done— at "the seminary" 'way back when he was a student there (though it's probably not that way now!); for others it is his cloudy image of the services in "the primitive Church" or in "the undivided Church."

But a moment's reflection will suggest that none of these norms can possibly have any finality— whether they date from the nineteenth century, or the 18th, 15th, 8th, or 3rd. The very fact that there are these various norms continually appealed to by respectable people within our Church would seem to rebut the eternalization of any one of the norms. And, in any case, to seek to finalize the historical is a form of idolatry.

So let's clear the decks. As to the form and number of ceremonies we use, God (whose worship it is) couldn't care less—apart from their communicability. To be more precise: He couldn't care less as to what hand-gestures a celebrant uses with his back to the people—which they don't see anyway. It's what the people see and hear and do that's important—not in itself, but for the sake of communication. Thus what ceremonies we use is entirely a relative matter—a pragmatic adaptation of means to an end.

But when I say that it is relative, I don't mean that it's unimportant. We belong to a Church which is committed to ceremonial presentation of the truth. And this isn't just a matter of custom. It is grounded in theology—in nothing less than the Doctrine of Creation. The material order is *good*, and can express, as well as be the means to, the spiritual. To use William Temple's phrase, this is "a sacramental universe." It may be that, in one sense, worship with little or no ceremonial is "more spiritual"; but our aim is not to be "more spiritual" but more sacramental. Not spirit rather than flesh; not substance rather than form. But spirit and flesh, substance and form, meaningfully related. Externals as means of expressing the internal and as "means of grace," i.e., of nourishing and refueling the things of the spirit.

Thus the *role* of form has a permanent validity. But no *particular* form does. The value of any such expression depends upon the truth of what is expressed and the satisfactoriness of the expression—taking into account those being communicated to, in a particular place and time.

The tests would seem to be these:

No matter how beautiful a ceremony or liturgical wording, it is not good if it teaches nothing. The service is over; the choir has marched out; the music softens—plus tremulo; two acolytes begin extinguishing candles—symmetrically; precisely when the last two are extinguished the organ booms, everyone immediately rises to depart. What does it mean? Something, doubtless, to Zoroastrian fire-worshippers. But what to Christians?

After the offertory sentence, six ushers walk solemnly up the aisle, an acolyte from the sanctuary joins them at the chancel steps and sorts out the alms basins. What does it mean? Can't we sufficiently trust the laity to arrange to have the basins at the back in the first place? Therefore:

1. *The ceremony should mean something.*

The following beautiful ceremony does mean something: a monstrance containing a large host is raised over the people, and the sign of the cross is made with it, as bells ring, incense is swung and acolytes fall to their faces. The meaning is clear: the reserved Sacrament is to be adored as such: transubstantiation. This doctrine our Church does not hold (*cf.* Article XXVIII). Therefore:

2. *What is meant by the ceremony should be true.*

The Epistle has been read; a server moves the book to the "Gospel" side. After the offertory sentence, the server brings to the celebrant the bread box and the cruets. These are jejeune remnants of two great processions: the Eastern Orthodox have always called them "the little entrance" and "the greater entrance." The first is a celebration of the coming of the Gospel into the world, and the second the celebration of the offering of all human life and activity to God. Whether one is "little" and the other "greater" would make an interesting theological discussion; but the fact is that the early Church expressed vividly the importance of these two things. This expression is not lost with us; the little ceremony of the moving of the book is almost universal in the Anglican Communion, and the requirement of the transportation of the oblations from some other place than the Altar to the Holy Table is obviously required by the third rubric on page 73 of the Prayer Book (though until recently, this requirement was universally fulfilled by a trip a few feet from the credence table to the Altar and rendered practically invisible by involvement of the congregation in putting their alms into the collection plates and by the activities of the choir). Happily, provision is now more generally being made for a real Gospel procession and a real offertory procession, with the oblations being brought up with the alms by members of the congregation, thus giving a proper and vigorous emphasis to the teachings underlying the ceremonies. Not even the most unalert member of the congregation can fail to take something of it in. Therefore:

3. *A ceremony should be bold—and evident as to its meaning.*

Throughout the Canon of the Eucharist some priests make various gestures over the oblations (for example, nine signs of the cross at the end of the Canon). Whatever these things may mean —in terms of some supposed tradition—to the celebrant himself, they are invisible to the congregation—and to the degree that they are observed from the rear they would suggest either nervousness on the part of the priest or some sort of esoteric voodoo. Nothing meaningful is communicated. Therefore:

4. *Ceremonies should not be too numerous to be "taken in" by the people, nor should they be private to the priest.*

The purpose of a ceremony should not be the satisfaction of the religious sensibilities of the cele-

brant, but *edification*. God could not care less
about our ceremonies, except insofar as they can
induce a meaningful response on the part of the
whole body. If it be objected that the priest is a
worshipper also and hence is entitled to do those
things which are helpful to his own worship, I
would answer that here we are talking about *public*
worship, not private spiritual exercises. Each task
when it comes to leading the congregation at worship is a public one, not a private one.

Up to this point, I have been discussing ceremonial in the light of its "preaching" capacity,
without particular reference to the effect of external actions on the unconscious mind. Now we
shall turn to that side of the matter. The "preached"
word, no matter how well-spoken or ill-spoken,
is generally received only on the conscious level.
But liturgy has a greater capacity for reaching
the unconscious mind as well. This is particularly
so where impressions therefrom can travel well-
worn channels. What might be good liturgy and
ceremonial if only conscious observation were involved, will not necessarily be equally apppropriate
in terms of reaching the unconscious with the
message of the Gospel.

And it is on this level we must act if the whole
man is to be reached. The fact is that a man's

mind is like an iceberg—eight-ninths under the surface. It is not enough that his conscious mind sees the logic of a particular doctrine or ethic; something must meet the challenge of compulsions arising from the unconscious which can frustrate or deflect the best images of the conscious mind. Hear St. Paul: "There is another law in my make-up that wars with the law in my mind; those things that I would do I don't seem able to do, and those things I would not do are the very things I find myself doing." One way toward the health of the unconscious is the constant injection of vivid symbols of the great meanings of our Faith.

This is a more difficult task than "teaching a lesson" to the conscious mind. To reach the unconscious, symbols must be "big and bold"; and they must have been repeated (for significant understanding in the conscious mind) frequently enough to have worn channels into the unconscious mind. Further, the whole atmosphere of worship should be such as to relieve the tensions and preoccupations which in the hours of our ordinary day-to-day life "keep the lid on" the unconscious mind, i.e., maintain a firm barrier between conscious and unconscious reception.

I think we can see this process by analyzing a simple familiar experience such as participation in the *Venite, exultemus Domino*. How carefully do people listen to the words of this invitatory psalm? I think that honest clergy and laity alike would admit that they only half listen to the words. Actually this is ideal. Nothing is more helpful for the successful communication to the unconscious of basic religious realities than a state of half-attention, half-inattention. This particular attitude is fostered by the use of chant. Its very monotony tends to relax the layer between the conscious and unconscious mind. (Gregorian chant is probably even better, because it is even more monotonous; it lacks a definite "meter" or rhythm.)

What as a result of injection into the unconscious is projected from it?

First, let's take the visions of Bernadette. This pious young girl believed she saw the Blessed Virgin Mary, labeled with the phrase I AM THE IMMACULATE CONCEPTION. The two obvious reactions to such a claim: the literal Roman Catholic would say that Mary was right there just as she appeared to be; the secularist or Protestant iconoclast would say "Not at all; sheer illusion." But there is another possible view of the matter. There is no question that something important—religiously important—happened to Bernadette: taking the whole story into account, it is apparent that her religion became more real to her, and there is no reason to suppose that this was not through the grace of God. The effect of this religious experience not at all unnaturally produced projections of images from the unconscious. Nor is it surprising that what was projected was conditioned by the statue of the Virgin Mary in her parish church, on which she had gazed many times—and intensively—in her prayers to the mother of our Lord. Nor is the "label" which the Virgin bore in the image surprising: around this time, before the declaration of the doctrine of the Immaculate Conception, the proposed doctrine was a matter of warm debate among theologians and other clergy; and those who had most influenced her thinking on the point were in favor of the doctrine. In other words, it is possible to recognize the reality of the experience without regarding the resulting projection as other than a "conditioned response."

In contrast, consider the high point of John Wesley's religious experience. After real failure in his Georgia ministry and his return to England he was seeking direction. As a member of a study group pondering Luther's commentary on the Epistle to the Romans he reports that "that night" about 9 o'clock in Aldersgate Street "I felt my heart strangely warmed." I doubt if a physician would have noted a rise in temperature. The externalization of what was going on in the whole of his being took form quite compatible with the evangelical studies in which he was engaged: had he been raised as Bernadette was, the projection might well have been that of the Virgin Mary (which might well have changed the whole course of Methodist devotional life!). The fact is that the experience was *real:* look at the results. This hitherto ineffectual person went out and preached thousands of sermons and changed the face of England—and, vicariously had a tremendous bearing on frontier America. We have every reason to trust the reality of the experience, and yet to be quite un-literal as to the particular form in which the experience was externally projected.

Enlightening too is a story Prof. A. T. Mollegen tells.

There was a woman office worker who always left her apartment at 8:30 in order to catch a certain bus. Living on the same floor was a gentleman on the night shift who always left the elevator at approximately 8:29. The result was that the elevator door was almost always still open, and so she was accustomed—without conscious thought—to stepping right in. One particular day there was a change. The man had taken the night off and the repair men were working on the elevator, the car being at the bottom floor—but by mistake the elevator door was still open above. Following her customary practice the lady walked right in—into an empty shaft. But suddenly she stepped back, in time to remain safe. She reported the incident to the manager and commented how fortunate it was that the janitor was right there to pull her back. He answered, *"It was the janitor's day off too."* Now if such a thing had occurred in the Middle Ages she might have reported that St. Michael was there to save her. But in our secular society it is not surprising that the *janitor* had become for her the symbol of security—for he was the one who was handy when needed. (This change is not exactly progress; there is more glory and mystery in a vision of St. Michael than in the vision of a flesh and blood employee!)

The point of these illustrations is that what is projected (without even conscious projection) rather depends in a large measure on what is injected. And yet spiritual *reality*—indeed Grace —may be the cause of the projection.

Now all through our days all kinds of unhealthy things are being injected into the unconscious. This is particularly so if we are not consistently solving our problems or resolving our conflicts on the conscious level, but rather are "hiding" them by rationalization or preoccupation or distraction —and letting them sink from the conscious level

to the unconscious level. The unconscious of most
of us is afflicted or burdened, in varying degrees,
by fears, guilts, hates and lusts. If these negative
and destructive things reach sufficient proportion
in their unconscious prison, they can take a person over, subduing the guards at the doors of the
prison and end up running the whole establish-
ment. At this point a real operation is called for:
some form of psychoanalysis and/or psychother-
apy.

But before things have reached this point any
sensible person who sees this developing problem
would want to take advantage of milder remedies.
In the purely physiological realm, operations are
sometimes necessary, but sometimes infection can
be cured by various types of rays focused from the
outside. By analogy: for most of us the operation
known as psychoanalysis may not be necessary;
but for many of us the internal contents of the
unconscious need the healing of the right kind
of rays from the outside, namely, the injection
into the unconscious of symbols of security, meaning, acceptance, and motivation to serve others.
The conscious mind can be told about all these
things through effective preaching—and this is
important. But the unconscious mind is better
reached by effective liturgical participation.

With this background sketched out, let us turn

to the *Venite* again and see what the content is, viewing it in the light of what health it can bring to the unconscious mind. Its phrases do not consist of rational argument, but of great and powerful images (oft reinforced by repetition) "O come, let us sing unto the Lord, the strength of our salvation": the source of our wholeness, our health. "For the Lord is a great God, a great King above all gods": this latter is not merely a reflection of primitive religion; but it does quite rightly assume the existence of other gods, i.e., foci with the power of domination.

In more ancient days these other gods were represented by statues and were given explicit names. The Baalim represented the emphasis on fertility: more crops, more flocks. (Today we simply worship "production" as an ideal.) The various gods (whether Venus, Ceres, Mammon, etc.) stood for good things, but things which could not be made the central focus of being, because everyone of them—or all taken together—could let you down (this is what the Bible means by "feet of clay"). The true God is a focus which can support all these other aims in a meaningful pattern—he will not let you down. We need not condemn—or destroy—the other gods; they will have a legitimate place in life if for us "He is the great King above all gods."

"In his hands are all the corners of the earth": there is no place you can go, no difficulty you can be in where He won't be there with you. "The strength of the hills is his also": He is more reliable than anything human or anything contrived. He is not merely an impersonal force. He cares —from his direction: "We are the people of his pasture, and the sheep of his hand": when we forget Him, He does not forget us ("If one sparrow . . ."). One sign of His care is the fact that He judges us. If we were lost in the Universe, just leaves blown by the wind, there would be no judgment: but "He cometh, he cometh to judge the earth, and with righteousness to judge the world and his peoples with his truth."

All this is very good for our inner health. These images speak to our need, and provide wholesome antibodies for the various feelings of fear, insecurity, isolation and inferiority so often resident in the unconscious mind.

All this is true of other parts of the liturgy and its external accompaniments. The words of the liturgy are generally not taken in phrase by phrase as though one were listening to a college lecture; the key ideas which have been heard over and over again are what make the impression. This gives a clue as to how the liturgy should be read. Obviously it should not be "rattled off" or mumbled, since it is not an incantation: it actually consists of intelligible sentences quite carefully thought out to state the truth soundly and in balance. On the other hand, it should not be "preached"—to "squeeze the juice" out of every word. This last way of reading it would be appropriate for a study class on the meaning of the liturgy, but its attempt to force intellectual analysis for each word and phrase interferes with worship; and such careful intellectual responses, even if achieved, might actually induce a barrier to the symbols of faith into the unconscious.

What is called for is a happy medium. The service, while not rushed, should be read "at a pretty good clip," in a direct intelligible tone without too great extremes in variance of pitch and not overly profound pauses. The tone should be neither casual nor eloquent. (Since so many of our clergy have been to the College of Preachers in Washington and thus heard its Warden celebrate, it will make my point clear for many if I say that Canon Theodore Otto Wedel has for me always represented the norm in this regard.)

But also effective in communication to the unconscious are the nonverbal symbols: the cross and torches passing in procession, altar lights, colors of the season, the basic sacramental means: bread, wine, water, oil—fundamental tokens of basic things.

The evidence of the way symbols and oft-heard

liturgical prayers reach the unconscious is provided by the experience many of us have had in hospital calls on semi-comatose patients. Cheerful comments and extemporary prayers will bring no reaction, but the Cross, the Host and Chalice placed before the eyes, often will arouse a response —as will familiar portions of the liturgy. (I have had the experience at the beginning of the Lord's Prayer of seeing the patient's lips move before the completion of it.) This is simply a more dramatic form of testifying to the relationship of our forms of worship on the unconscious minds of people participating in the regular services.

The reality of communication with the liturgy to the unconscious thus has, as suggested above, a bearing on the way the liturgy should be performed and has a more fundamental bearing than considerations of "high" or "low" church. So far we have been talking about the "how" of communication by this means. Now we should turn to the "what." We know the "propers," i.e., the rounds of antiphons, psalms, lections, collects, Epistles, Gospels and proper prefaces—which obviously communicate specific ideas. Apart from these, what is the shape of the liturgy, and how does it communicate?

Throughout the Judeo-Christian tradition there have been two basic services of worship. One is the service of the word and the other is a service of action. The first is the service of the synagogue (thus in Greek it is called *synaxis*); the second is a sacramental service based on both the Jewish home service and on the service at the temple at Jerusalem. *Both* seek to communicate the continuing revelation of God and to involve the participants, through prayer, praise and action, in its implications. One relies more on the use of words—both hearing them and singing or saying them; the other relies more on involvement with Holy Things.

Throughout the history of the tradition these two have not always been kept in balance. Some traditions at some periods have had a heavy emphasis on the Sacrament and neglected the word; other traditions for given periods had limited sacramental observances to infrequent occasions and put virtually all the emphasis on the word. The early Church kept the two services in good balance. They continued synagogue worship and also continued the Jewish family service which since we have called the Lord's Supper.

The synagogue service became much more complicated through the influence of the monasteries; the people were left out of more and more of the service; this became particulaly so when Latin became less and less the language of the common people—no longer really the "vulgate."

In our own English Reformation, in order to restore a participating emphasis in the service of the word, the choir offices were simplified and put in the language of the people. It is true that our Eucharistic rite contains a brief *synaxis*, but it is much too jejune and, except for a few days a year, lacks an Old Testament lection and does very little by way of praise of God, the celebration of Creation and of the Providence of God and the recital of Holy History.

The architect of our Prayer Book, Archbishop Cranmer, assumed that both Morning Prayer and Holy Communion would be utilized; hence no attempt was made in the Eucharist alone to provide a "balanced diet" as far as the communication of the Faith is concerned. But as things developed the two services have become separated, with different congregations at each—and in fact with the majority of Episcopalians taking part, at most, in three services of Matins and one Eucharist a month. But neither service alone provides an adequate vehicle for the communication of the mighty acts of God and for the involvement of people in them.

To start with the Eucharist: apart from pages devoted to variable items (i.e., the proper collects, epistles and gospels, proper prefaces and the variable offertory sentences), nine of the main thirteen pages have a heavy concentration on sin and the Atonement. Now these are of course very important themes. And our Eucharistic rite is *historically* right in reflecting the heavy emphasis on them both in the late Middle Ages and in the Reformation period. But to see that this is by no means the whole of our Faith we have only to turn to Morning Prayer with its strong emphasis on the doctrines of Creation and Providence—and God's working in history. And there is a richer development (through the changing psalms and lessons and the prayers) of man's vocation under God and its applicable implications. There is not lacking coverage of the themes of sin and Atonement; but in this service there is not as vivid a personal confrontation and call for decision as there is in the Eucharist, since in a choir office the person present is not called upon to *do* anything. The table service is consummated in actually "going up" to Communion; thus it requires—or ought to require—an actual facing of one's sins, repentance for them and a firm purpose of amendment. It is possible to avoid this confrontation even at a Eucharist—either by not going to Communion or going heedlessly (see the Second Exhortation, never read these days); but it is much easier to do so at Morning Prayer. To put it more vividly, at the latter service a man continuing to keep a mistress or run a crooked business can easily continue so to do with some degree of complacency (though we will all grant that it is an illogical complacency). He can praise God for the beauties of the earth; be edified by the recital of Holy History, attend to prayers for those in need, and thank God for His many blessings. He cannot so easily, without a change in his intentions, participate in the Sacrament.

This is doubtless one reason (though by no means the only reason) why many laymen, including those whose sins are by no means as vivid as those chosen for the examples, prefer Morning Prayer as the normal Sunday service. Another is that our American eucharistic rite is too long, for two reasons: (1) revision is blocked by our General Convention and (2) unlike most of the rest of the Anglican Communion, with us laymen may not assist in the distribution of the Sacrament. But it is quite evident from the Bible, from the unbroken practice of the Church until the Reformation and from the views of *all* of the Reformers that the Lord's Supper is normative for the principal service.

And the Prayer Book makes clear that it *is* the principal service. Yet it is evident that there is an imbalance in teaching if it is the *only* service

celebrated at the main hour. Therefore it is not
enough to settle the question by simply referring
to the Eucharist as "our Lord's own service." It
can be said with equal truth, though in a different
sense, that Morning Prayer is "our Lord's own
service." While the Supper is the service He insti-
tuted (or perhaps more correctly, which He en-
dorsed with a deeper meaning), the Matins prayer
type of service is what He was raised on as He
attended the synagogue.

So the answer would seem to be both/and,
not either/or. This point has been perceived by
the draftsman of the Liturgy of the Church of
South India and by various reformed or proposed
liturgies of the Anglican Communion (but apparently not by the draftsmen of our own proposed
American Eucharist).

All that I have said in particular in regard to the
proper "shape of the liturgy" (to use Dom Gregory
Dix's book-title) is not meant to suggest practical
arrangements for a given parish. Indeed as bishop
I have often asked a given vicar not to disturb the
existing order in one regard or another, simply
because what the given vicar has in mind—and
what I see as an ideal—would not "go" in a
given place at this given time. My analysis has
been meant simply as a catalytic agent. The point

is that conscious thought should be given to each thing being done—with careful attention, *inter alia,* to the maximum possibilities of liturgy as communication.

In doing this, the person immediately in charge of public worship should, prayerfully and thoughtfully, consider various factors: (1) what is ideally right? (2) what is this congregation ready for? (what it is ready for at a given time will depend upon the kinds of preaching and instruction and postoral relationship that have been going on); (3) will a new approach *now* (not last year or next year—*now*) contribute to the communication of the Gospel?

As I close on this topic, I say this in regard to liturgy: my notions on it are certainly not final —nor are yours. But *use* the liturgy to manifest the Gospel. And, speaking more broadly, I say: use everything (even be "a fool for Christ's sake," as St. Paul was willing to be) to communicate the Faith *now*.

INDEX

Freshness is an important part of Bishop Pike's emphasis when presenting the Christian faith. He believes that the communication of the gospel calls for modern methods and he shows in these pages how the science of modern merchandising can be helpful. Much preaching, he says, errs either in presenting the real thing in a way nobody cares about, or in levelling off everything so that answers are in no higher terms than the questions asked. The book opens with a discussion of what has been happening to people in this age of transition, then the author explains what we are trying to communicate and how this can best be done in the light of our changing times, and finally he considers the context of preaching with its relation to the service as a whole.

Bishop Pike quotes the old adage that the purpose of preaching is to comfort the afflicted and to afflict the comfortable.

This book is based on the George Craig Stewart Memorial Lectures on Preaching at Seabury-Western Theological Seminary.